MY OWN FUN

Creative Learning Activities for Home and School, Ages 7–12

Carolyn Buhai Haas and
Anita Cross Friedman

Chicago Review Press

To Ben Friedman; Lisa and Courtney Haas; Alexis and Zachary Rubin; Rachael, Molly, and Spencer Beckert; Nicholas Foletta; Allison Leigh McNier; and Danielle Friedman

Library of Congress Cataloging-in-Publication Data

Haas, Carolyn.
     My own fun: creative learning activities for home and
school / Carolyn Buhai Haas and Anita Cross Friedman.
     —1st ed.
     p.   cm.
     Includes bibliographical references.
     ISBN 1-55652-093-X : $9.95
     1. Activity programs in education—Handbooks, manuals, etc.
     2. Teaching—Aids and devices—Handbooks, manuals, etc.
     I. Friedman, Anita Cross.   II. Title.
     LB1027.25.H33   1990
     371.3'078—dc20   90-44181
                                                          CIP

First edition

   2   3   4   5   6   7   8   9   10

Printed in the United States of America

Published by Chicago Review Press, Incorporated
814 N. Franklin Street
Chicago, IL 60610

ISBN 1-55652-093-X

Contents

Acknowledgments   ix
Introduction   xi
Handy To Save   xiii
Handy To Buy   xiv

Crayons and Paint   1
    Super Crayon Sticks   2
    Melted Crayon Shapes   2
    Sandy Crayon Designs   3
    Sidewalk Chalk Sticks   4
    Gesso Paint   5
    Gesso Modeling Compound   6
    Thick Frosty Paint   6
    Foam Paint   6
    Window-Painting   7
    Ice Crystal Pictures   7
    Dribble Designs   7
    Framing and Displaying Your Art   8

Papercraft   11
    Animals   12
    Masks   12
    Gift Boxes and Bags   12
    Shimmery Wrapping Paper   13
    Pop-Up Place Cards   14
    Star Shapes   14
    Paper Snowflakes   15
    Dip-and-Dye Snowflakes   16
    Hundreds of Hats   16
    Paper Flowers   18
    Paper Boat   19
    Magic Sailboats   21
    Be a Boat Builder   22
    Spider Webs   24
    House of Cards   26

Pastes and Putties   29
    Thin Paste   30
    Library Paste   30
    Cornstarch Paste   31
    Glutin Chips   32
    Glue   32
    Transparent Glue   33
    Casein Glue   33

Flexible Forms   34
Rubber Cement Eraser   34
Toothpaste Putty   35
Silly Putty   35
Plastic Gel   36

Modeling Compounds   37

Papier-Mâché Mash   38
Colorful Soap Dough   38
Sand Dough   39
Dryer Lint Dough   40
Sawdust Modeling Compound Relief Map   40
Plaster Ghosts, Angels, and Tunnel Shapes   41
Plaster of Paris Sculpture in a Bag   42
Soap Crayons   43
Soft Soap Carving   44
Natural Clay Modeling   45
Ceramic Clay Tiles   47

Dyeing, Sewing, and Weaving   51

Japanese Shibori Designs   52
Native American Natural Dyes   53
Sunshine Dyes   55
Tie-and-Fade Dyeing   55
Wearable Art   56
Stitchery   57
Weaving   59

Photography and Optics   63

Make a Pinhole Camera   64
Nighttime Experiment   66
Sun Pictures   66
Chalkboard Photography   67
Make a Viewfinder   68
Rose-Colored Glasses   69
Giant Kaleidoscope   70
Triple Disk Kaleidoscope   71
Optical Illusions   73

Kitchen Chemistry   77

Magic Pennies   78
Vanishing Acts   78
Hidden Colors   78
Changing Colors   79
Flower Petals   79
Indicator Sticks   80
The Columbus Egg   80

Sugar Magic   81
Sugar Crystals   81
Sticky Bubbles   83

Wind and Weather   85

Simple Weather Vane   86
Wind Anemometer   87
Rain Gauge   88
Make a Water Windmill   89
Weather Myths   92
Experiments in Aerodynamics   92
Parachutes   93
Paper Airplane Race   93

Kites   97

Bow-and-Arrow Bird Kite   98
Grocery Bag Kite   99
Drinking Straw Kite   100
Basic Diamond-Shaped Kite   101
Kite Festival   102
Other Facts About Kites   103
Japanese Kites   103

Gardening and Nature   105

Vegetable and Flower Garden   106
Unusual Plants   107
Hanging Gourds   108
Windowsill or Flower Pot Garden   108
Bottle Scoop   110
Plant Water Bottle   110
Pretty Potato Face   110
Autumn Nature Walk   111
Seeing the Forest Through the Trees   112
Camouflaged Nature Hunt   114
Visit a Botanical Garden   115

Birds and Animals   117

Birdhouse   118
A Bluebird House   118
Robin's Roost   119
Nests   119
Feeding the Birds   120
Milk Carton Feeder   120
Automatic Feeder   122
Bird Watching   122
The World Series of Bird Watching   123
Bird and Animal Guessing Games   124

Zoo Cards   126
Zoo-Ography   126
Endangered Species   127
The Piping Plover   129

Sea and Land   131

The Sea Shore   132
Beach Games   132
Cut the Cake   132
Sand Pictures   133
Active Games   133
Seagull and Sandpipers   134
Rock Creatures   134
Mermaids and Other Sea Creatures   135
Starfish   135
Rock Pots   136
Build an Oceanarium   136
Be a Nautical Archaeologist   138
Mock Volcano   140
Make a Dinosaur Fossil   141
Fossil Bones and Other Objects   143

What's in a Name?   145

Name Research   146
Nicknames   147
Towns and Counties   147
Name Poems   148
My Name Is   149
Silly Sentences   149
Name Signs   149
Celebrity Names   150

Outdoor Games   151

Giant Chain Tag   152
Tommy Can't Cross the Sea   152
Celebrity Stoop Tag   152
Tricky Dancers   153
Have a Ball   153
Leisure Time   155

Games from Other Countries   157

Catch the Tail   158
The Big Snake (Da Ga)   159
Jumping the Beanbag (Africa)   159
Chinese Chuck Stone   159
Flipball (Greece, China, and Mexico)   160
Chinese Shuttlecock   160

Ring and Pin Game   161

Board Games and Timers   163
African Kahla or Wari   164
Nine Men's Morris   165
Stopwatch Fun   166
Homemade Timers   167
Bottle-Up   167
Simple Water Timer   168
Water Timer Extravaganza   169

New in the 1990s   171
From 1890 to 1990   172
The Year 2040   173
Be an Inventor   174
A Century of Telephones   175
Solar Energy   180
TV's 50th Birthday   182

Resources   189

Acknowledgments

Special thanks to our editors, Linda Matthews and Mary Munro; Alexis Rubin, Karen Haas-Foletta, Herbert Weissman, Cissy Haas, Larry Clampitt, Stephen B. Friedman, Sylvia and Alfred Friedman, Norma and Bill Buckman, Carol Felsenthal, Millie Cross, Linda Cummens, Sally Ward, Ann Cole, Elizabeth Heller, and Betty Weinberger; and the many friends, relatives, authors, and librarians who helped guide and enrich this book.

We are also indebted to current newspapers and magazine articles found in *Smithsonian*, *National Geographic*, *Time*, *Newsweek*, *USA Today*, *US News & World Report*, and *Sunset* for many of the up-to-the-minute activities and projects.

Introduction

Welcome to *My Own Fun*, a sourcebook overflowing with creative and innovative learning activities for use at home or in the classroom. Children of all ages, but especially those in second through seventh grade, will find hundreds of challenging projects based on inexpensive or "saved" materials, an easy-to-follow format, and an abundance of appealing and instructive illustrations.

Like its predecessor, this volume covers a wide scope of interests, including unusual arts and crafts ideas, challenging nature and science projects (with emphasis on the new technologies of the nineties), indoor and outdoor games, and much, much more!

All of the activities are fun, easy-to-do, and up-to-the-minute in content. They can be enjoyed by one child alone, a small group, the entire family, or a classroom of kids. All are designed to expand a child's horizons and to encourage creative thinking, problem solving, and cooperative learning—all of utmost importance in today's ever-changing world.

Readers can browse through the pages, picking out one or two projects to try; or they can tackle an entire section for a more in-depth approach. There is sure to be something for everyone, from the brand-new to the tried-and-true, whether it be creating a futuristic telephone or a drinking-straw kite; a glow-in-the-dark clipboard or homemade dyes from flower petals, walnut shells, and purple grapes; an elaborate relief map or model oceanarium.

"Add-ons" suggest ways of easily expanding and enriching the projects and adapting them to various times and occasions. The extensive Resource section invites further exploration, creativity, and knowledge.

So open up the pages and enjoy the many delights that await you in *My Own Fun*!

Handy To Save

Containers

oatmeal, cornmeal, and grits cartons
margarine tubs
berry baskets
egg cartons
boxes and cans of all sizes
cardboard, styrofoam grocery trays
cardboard tubes from toilet tissue, paper towels, and hangers

Scraps of . . .

paper
ribbon
yarn
string
wrapping paper

Odds and Ends

buttons
spools
jar lids
popsicle sticks
paper plates and cups
feathers, rocks
bottle caps
keys, corks
straws
toothpicks
styrofoam

Don't Forget

newspapers
magazines
paper bags of all sizes
shirt cardboards

Handy To Buy

crayons, pencils, chalk
scissors, X-Acto knife
hole puncher
brad fasteners
sponges
white glue/paste
resin glue
metal rings
Q-tips
masking, transparent, and cloth tape
watercolor, tempera, textile, and/or acrylic paints
felt tip markers
clear contact paper
paper of all kinds: construction, typing, shelf, newsprint, crepe, and tissue
tag board
colored cellophane, aluminum foil
food coloring, rainbow foam paints
sewing materials
plastic zip bags
There are many exciting new art materials on the market that you may wish to try. Just visit a hobby or craft store, and take your pick!

Helpful Hints

1. Buy only the essentials! Try to save as many usable items as you can.
2. A few minutes of preplanning can lead to hours of challenging and constructive play.
3. It is not the completed product that is the most important, but the process of learning through doing, exploring, problem solving, and creating.
4. Children love to be praised for a job well done. Success-oriented experiences are very important.

A Note on Safety

Safety is a "must" at all times. Children ten and older need the experience of using the kitchen stove and tools such as hammers, saws, and the X-Acto knife, but they also need instruction and supervision as they learn. An adult should supervise every activity in which cooking or cutting with a sharp knife is involved. Younger children should look on as an adult does the cooking and cutting. Teach your children to ask for the help they need—and be ready to help them when they ask.

CRAYONS AND PAINT

Super Crayon Sticks

YOU NEED:

Old candles or paraffin wax

1 teaspoon turpentine (for older kids only) or linseed oil

3 tablespoons powdered paint

Paper towel tube or juice can

YOU DO:

1. Cut up old candles or paraffin wax and weigh out 1 ounce.

2. Put the wax in an old tin can and set it in pan of water on low heat until the wax melts. Ask an adult to help you.

3. Remove the can (use a hot pad) from the heat and stir in the powdered paint with a stick or old spoon.

4. Cover one end of a paper towel tube with foil or waxed paper, or use the juice can, and carefully pour in the wax. Repeat for individual colors, or experiment with layers of color.

5. When the wax hardens, just peel off the tube, or use it as a handy crayon wrapper.

6. Have fun coloring with your giant crayon!

ADD-ONS:

Experiment with a variety of different molds for your homemade crayons. Tin cigar cases or plastic toothbrush holders will make tall, thin crayons; a muffin tin will produce 6 or 8 round, fat ones.

Melted Crayon Shapes

YOU NEED:

Old crayons, waxed paper

Vegetable grater or potato peeler

Newspapers, iron, tape

YOU DO:

1. Peel off the wrappers from the crayons; separate them into the same or similar colors.

2. Shave the crayons and store the shavings in an egg carton or small containers to keep the colors separate.

3. Cut 2 pieces of waxed paper into shapes (circle, star, diamond, apple, holiday symbols, etc.). Sprinkle piles of crayon shavings on top of 1 piece, being sure to leave a border of waxed paper. Then cover your design with the second shape. (You could use only one color or several, as long as you don't use *opposite* colors to muddy the design.)

4. Place the waxed paper design on top of a pile of newspapers, cover with several more newspapers, and gently press over the paper with a warm iron. Ask an adult to help with this.

5. Reinforce the edges with tape, or frame your shapes with 2 cut-out cardboard shapes a little smaller than the waxed paper, and hang them up in the window to catch the sun.

Sandy Crayon Designs

YOU NEED:

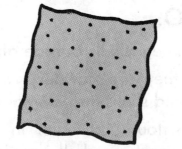

Sheets of fine sandpaper
Crayons, foil

YOU DO:

1. Press down on your crayons hard, as you color in a design or picture on the sandpaper.

2. To make straight and wavy crayon lines, peel the paper off a few crayons, and cut out 2 or 3 V-shaped notches along one side. You could also bundle a few crayons together with rubber bands and press with the tips to make multiple lines.

3. Cover a cookie sheet with foil; place the sandpaper picture on it, and bake in a preheated 250° oven (on the middle rack) for 2 or 3 minutes, until the crayon melts. You could also use a warming plate. Note: Always wear oven mitts when working with something hot.

ADD-ONS:

Use this same method with other materials: paper, cardboard, wood for colorful crayon pictures. Wash black tempera paint over the crayoned surface, and scratch in designs to make crayon etchings. Use this method to make bookmarks, placemats, and ocean scenes.

Sidewalk Chalk Sticks

This kind of chalk works fine on concrete, but not very well on a regular chalkboard. Make the chalk outdoors, and you won't have much mess to worry about.

YOU NEED:

4–6 washed and dried eggshells

1 teaspoon flour

1 teaspoon tap water (very hot)

YOU DO:

1. Take the eggshells outside and smash them with a smooth rock.

2. When they are powdery, throw away any large pieces, and scoop the powdered shells into a small bowl or dish.

3. Put the flour and water in another bowl, mix into a paste, then add 1 teaspoon of eggshell powder. Keep mashing until the mixture sticks together.

4. Put the dough into your hand and roll it into a chalk stick shape. Wrap it tightly with a strip of paper toweling.

5. Let the chalk stick dry for 2 or 3 days until it is very hard. Then use it on the sidewalk to draw pictures or play hop scotch and other games. Use the bottom of your shoe, or the next hard rain, as an eraser!

Gesso Paint

YOU NEED:

1 teaspoon white glue

1 tablespoon dextrin solution—ask your druggist (commercial gesso from an art store could be substituted)

Powdered chalk or patching plaster

Acrylic paints

Items to be decorated (small wooden box, picture frame, bookends, etc.)

YOU DO:

1. To make the dextrin solution, dissolve 1 cup of powdered dextrin in a tablespoon of hot water. Add the teaspoon of glue.

2. Pour 1 tablespoon of the dextrin and glue solution in a bowl (save the rest in a covered jar to use at another time), and add the chalk or patching powder. Mix into a thick paste that can be applied with a brush.

3. Draw a design or a pattern on the item you want to decorate. Using a brush or a cake decorator, fill in the design with your gesso paint until it is the height you want it.

4. Let the gesso dry, then color in with acrylic paints.

ADD-ONS:

You can also carve the gesso with a small, sharp knife. To make small shapes, holiday designs, numbers, alphabet letters, etc., form the gesso on a piece of waxed paper. Allow to dry, then lift off and glue onto a hard surface for a decoration. You could make nifty name plates and house number signs with this paint.

Gesso Modeling Compound

To make a gesso modeling compound (enough for 2 or 3 small objects: fruit, flowers, holiday shapes, and so forth), substitute ¼ cup patching plaster, powdered chalk, unscented talcum powder, or plaster of paris for the glue, and add it to the dextrin solution. Mix it in a tablespoon at a time, with a stick or a putty or palette knife. Knead the mixture together for several minutes until pliable and claylike. Let dry for about a week before painting. To preserve the artwork, brush or spray on shellac.

Thick Frosty Paint

YOU NEED:

> 1 cup powdered tempera
>
> 2 tablespoons wallpaper paste
>
> Liquid laundry starch
>
> Paintbrush, cardboard, or
>   popsicle stick for spreading

YOU DO:

Mix the tempera and wallpaper paste. Add ¼ to ½ cup liquid laundry starch and mix until the paint is stiff as frosting. Use a stubby paintbrush, a piece of cardboard, or a popsicle stick to apply the paint to paper, cardboard, or glass.

Foam Paint

Whip up some Ivory Snow and a little water with an eggbeater or wire whisk. Add regular or powdered tempera paint. Place a dab on a window, paper, or your bathtub, and you're all ready to fingerpaint!

Window-Painting

YOU NEED:

Thick Frosty Paint or Foam Paint

A window

YOU DO:

1. Get permission to decorate a window to look like frost or to make a colortul picture with your frosty paints.

2. Cover the window with paint. Then use your fingers to make a design or a picture.

3. Use crumpled newspapers to remove the pictures and your window will be sparkling clean!

Ice Crystal Pictures

Crayon a design on a dark piece of construction paper, pushing down hard on the crayons. Then "paint" over the picture with a solution of equal parts of Epsom salts and water. Wait and see what happens.

Dribble Designs

1. Squeeze out or dribble paint onto a piece of construction paper. Use several colors.

2. For an even more exciting effect, fold the paper in half and smooth over it with your hand. Open it up and your multi-colored Rorschach design will appear.

3. Hold the paper under a slowly dripping faucet, and let the water make a design on it.

4. Then take your paints, colored pencils, or chalk and go over the lines and splotches of the design. The paints will run together and make a lovely picture.

Framing and Displaying Your Art

There are many ways to frame your works of art, ranging from very easy to complicated. Here are some suggestions:

Colored Construction Paper

1. Glue your picture on a larger sheet of construction paper, or fold a sheet of paper and cut out a rectangle to make a frame. A wavy cut-out frame is even more fun.

2. Glue strips of contrasting or similar colors in bands on the 4 sides of your picture.

3. Fold a piece of paper in half and glue your picture inside for a card. For a standing frame, glue the picture to the outside.

Cardboard, Posterboard, or Tagboard

1. Glue pictures onto the board, or cut out the inside to make a mat. You may need an adult to help with the cutting.

2. Glue wallpaper, wrapping paper, or construction paper shapes onto cardboard frames. Add colorful yarn, paste, beads, glitter, etc., for more interest.

3. Paper plates, pizza rounds, paper grocery bags with cut-out "windows" provide unusual frames. Flatten the bags or suspend them from the ceiling as picture mobiles.

4. Box lids, facial tissue, and other boxes also work well.

5. Giant cut-out letters and shapes (including holiday ones) make excellent frames for groups of pictures.

Vinyl Placemats, Wide Ribbons, Scrap Fabric Material

1. Old or new placemats in a variety of colors can be used as is to frame your art, or cut them up into interesting shapes.

2. Hang a group of pictures from wide ribbons or colorful fabric.

3. To create hang-ups, sew a seam along the top and bottom edges of a piece of burlap or other fabric. Insert a wooden dowel, tree branch, cardboard tube from a wire hanger, or paper towel tube.

4. Create art mobiles out of cardboard shapes, tree branches, etc.

5. Attach paintings to a rope or ribbon with clip clothespins.

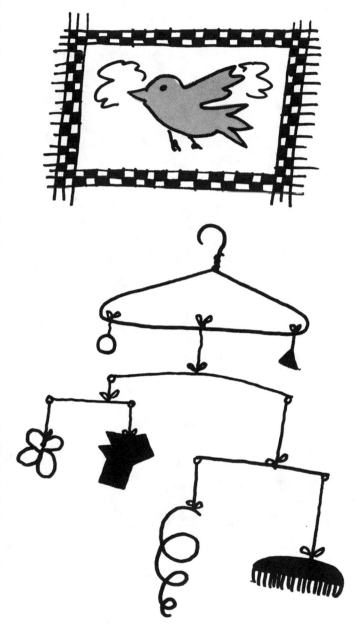

Large Boxes and Cartons

1. Display sculpture, clayworks, and small pieces of art on decorated or covered boxes. Stack some for variety. A painted orange crate or a sturdy wooden ladder also provide good display space.

2. Make a 4-sided giant frame by cutting shapes into the sides of a large box.

Permanent Art Displays

1. Secure a large tree branch in a bucket of sand or plaster for a year-long, changeable display.

2. Suspend artwork from a netting of 6-pack holders, rope, or mesh material.

3. Don't forget the old standby—bulletin boards. Use your ingenuity to dream up other ways of displaying works of art.

PAPERCRAFT

There are so many things you can make with paper, scissors, glue, and felt tip markers.

Animals

1. Form the heads and bodies from colorful construction paper cylinders and cones of various sizes. Roll, fold, and fringe small pieces of paper for tails, legs, paws, fins, feathers, horns, beaks, eyes, mouths, teeth, or whatever you can dream up.

2. Use colored markers to put on the finishing touches.

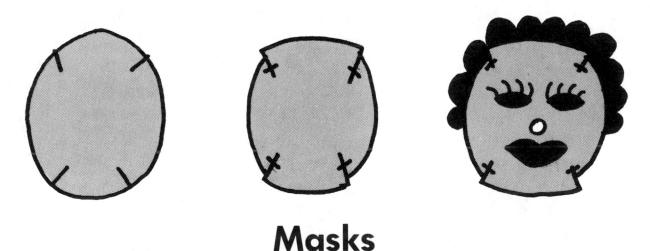

Masks

1. To make a 3-dimensional mask from a single piece of paper, start with a basic oval mask shape.

2. Make 2 cuts at the top of the oval and 2 more at the bottom. Now you have a tab or flap at the top and the bottom of the mask.

3. Overlap each tab edge with the edge of the mask and tape or staple firmly. Now your mask is 3-dimensional.

4. Cut out, fold, and/or roll paper scraps for features. Cut out a mouth and put in teeth. Fringe eyelashes and hair and add a hat, glasses, eyebrows, lips, and whatever else you can think of.

5. A good way to attach small parts is to cut tabs for them and insert them through slits in the mask, gluing or taping them down from behind.

Gift Boxes and Bags

1. Cover boxes of various sizes with construction paper and decorate with shapes, holiday symbols, curlicues, sculptured flowers, and so forth.

2. Do the same thing with paper bags and shopping bags.

3. For an added effect, tie with colorful yarn or ribbon.

Shimmery Wrapping Paper

1. Create shimmery wrapping paper by covering sheets of aluminum foil with scraps of colorful tissue paper, glued down by acrylic polymer and water.

2. Make several layers, if you wish. The result will be heavy, shiny paper that will dazzle your family and friends!

Pop-Up Place Cards

1. Fold a piece of paper or cardboard lengthwise.
2. Unfold, and write the person's name along the folded edge. (Script letters are the best, but printed ones also can be used.)
3. Thicken the name by drawing a line around the script that echoes the contour of the words, as in the illustration.
4. Poke the tip of your scissors in and cut along the top line, being sure to leave both ends of the fold line attached.
5. Bend the card back along the fold and the name will pop out! Decorate your place card, if you wish.

ADD-ONS:

You could also draw and cut out animals, toys, holiday symbols, etc., instead of names. It isn't necessary to do step 3, since the objects are big enough to stand up when cut.

Star Shapes

Draw and cut out paper or cardboard stars of various sizes.

1. Decorate them with marking pens, glitter, or paint, or cover the shapes with foil. Suspend them from the ceiling.
2. Punch holes in cardboard stars and glue colored cellophane behind, or flash a light through. Sew yarn or colorful shoelaces through the holes. (To make a tip on the

yarn, wrap on tape or dip the ends in nail polish.)

3. Make a star book by cutting out large star-shaped pages and a cover. Staple the pages together or punch holes and loop some yarn through.

4. Dip cardboard or styrofoam stars into tempera paint and use them to make star prints. Cut the painted stars up to make puzzles.

5. Of course, store-bought star stickers are the easiest of all, but that's only if you can't think of ways to make your own.

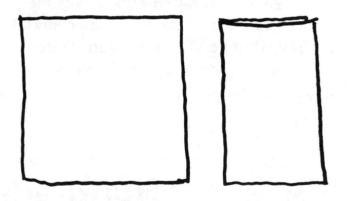

Paper Snowflakes

1. Fold a square of white paper in half; then fold up the corners to the center, as shown in illustration.

2. Fold once more into a triangular shape and cut out designs along the folded edges.

3. Open up the paper and you will have a beautiful lacy snowflake!

Dip-and-Dye Snowflakes

1. Use coffee filters or white paper towels and napkins to fold and cut snowflakes.

2. Dip the ends of the paper triangles into batches of colored dye or food coloring. Open up and let your multi-colored flakes dry. Hang up or use as doilies and other decorations.

3. Try doing this with different sizes, shapes, and varieties of paper. It's a little like fabric tie-dying.

4. For lacy placemats, fold a piece of construction paper in half and then in half again. (Do this again to make even more intricate designs.) Then make cuts along the edges. Open up the paper and see what you have created. Decorate the placemats, or leave them as is.

Hundreds of Hats

A creative hat is just the thing to get you into the dress-up mood. Change the hat and you can be anyone you want, from a gourmet chef to a Halloween witch. Here are just a few ideas to get you started.

Newspaper Hats

Fold, cut, and tape newspapers of various sizes into hat shapes. Comic pages are particularly colorful. Other newspaper pages create interesting effects, too (pictures, ads, large and small type, etc.). It's fun to vary the paper as well as the design of the hat.

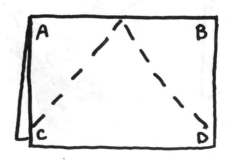

Try folding a newspaper or construction paper hat according to the instructions below.

1. Fold a large piece of newspaper or construction paper in half and smooth over the crease. With the folded edge at the top, turn corners A and B into the middle and then almost to the bottom.

2. Next, fold the open edge (from C to D) up; turn over and fold up the other edge. You now have a soldier's hat.

3. To make a sturdier hat, turn the soldier's hat upside down and gently bring corners C and D together. Flatten this diamond shape firmly.

4. Turn corner C down to X and smooth it out. Turn the hat over and do the same with corner D. Now you have a sturdy Dutch hat. Decorate it to suit your fancy.

Witch's Hat

Fold and tape a large piece of black construction paper into a cone to fit your head. Next, cut out a large brim to match. Cut tabs in the top edge of the brim and glue, tape, or staple them to the cone. Attach yarn hair if you wish.

Fashionable Chapeaux

For a fancy hat to go with your dress-up or garden clothes, fashion a paper hat with a large brim. This is an excellent outdoor art activity for a warm, sunny day.

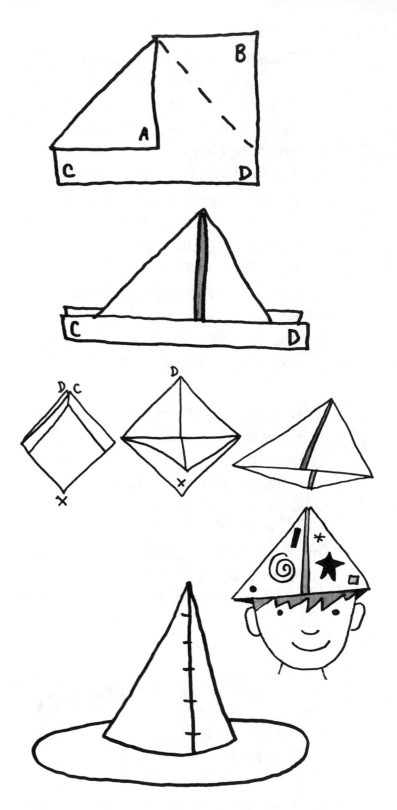

1. Cover a large square of colorful gift wrap paper with white glue diluted with water. Place a second square over the first, and brush on more glue.

2. Ask a friend to mold the damp paper to your head for a crown; then tie a string or ribbon tightly around it. The extra paper will form the brim.

3. Let the hat dry on your head for about 10 minutes; then remove it and gently pull it into the shape you want. Allow it to dry thoroughly.

4. Decorate your hat with paint (sunshine dyes would be perfect!), paper flowers, ribbons, colorful cutouts, or whatever pleases you.

ADD-ONS:

This would be a good papier-mâché project too. After you have formed the crown and brim, layer strips of newspaper dipped in mâché glue over the hat shape, and you will have a really sturdy hat that will last a long time.

Paper Flowers

1. Tissue and crepe paper make beautiful paper flowers. Just cut out 3 or 4 circles, and bunch them together on a wire or a pipe cleaner.

2. Cut or flute the edges, add leaves, and cover the wire stems with strips of green crepe paper.

3. Another way: Ruffle the edges of strips of crepe paper by putting your forefinger and middle finger on the strip and pushing the paper up between them with the forefinger of your other hand, as in illustration. Wind the ruffled strips around a finger or a pencil to make a rose or other flower.

Paper Boat

If you can fold a paper hat, you are on your way to making a boat as well. It's great fun to make a whole fleet in all different colors and sizes.

1. Fold a piece of paper (typing, construction, or newspaper) in half and smooth over the crease. With the folded edge at the top, turn corners A and B into the middle and then almost to the bottom.

2. Next, fold the open edge (from C to D) up; turn over and fold up the other edge.

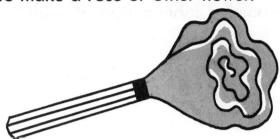

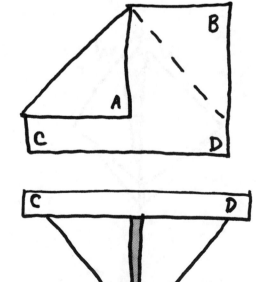

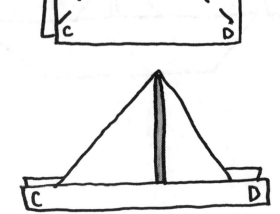

3. Turn this shape upside down and gently bring corners C and D together. You now have a diamond shape. Smooth it down firmly.

4. Turn corner C down to X and smooth it. Turn the shape over and do the same with corner D. Now you have a triangle.

5. Pull open at E and flatten into a small double-triangle or diamond shape, as you did in step 3. This diamond, though, is smaller.

6. Turn the diamond so the opening is at the bottom. Pull out at W on both sides of the diamond, pushing the sides up with your thumbs. Crease well at the bottom. Put your fingers inside the pointed cabin to open it a little. Your paper boat is all set to sail!

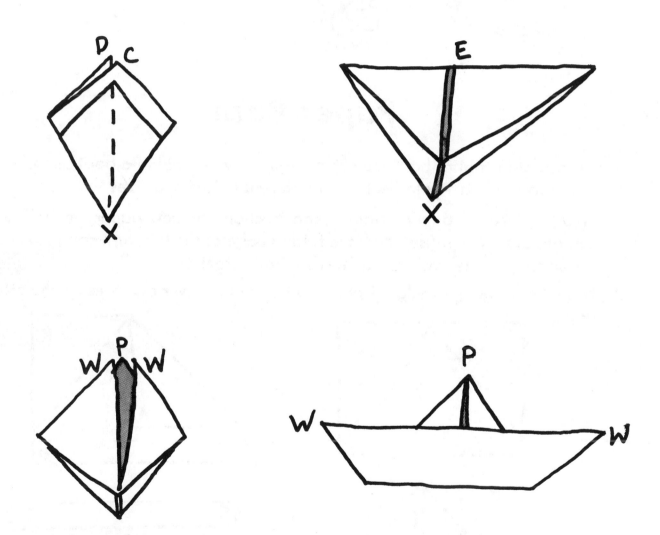

Magic Sailboats

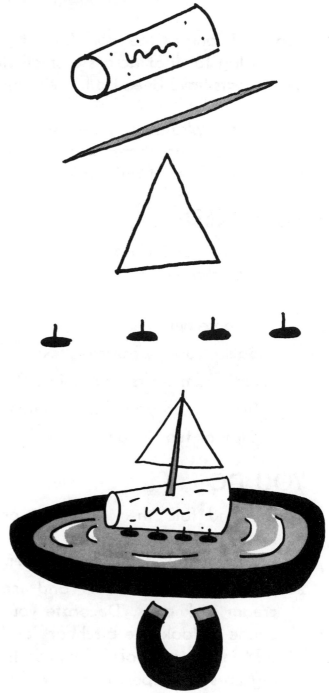

YOU NEED:

A cork, 4 or 5 tacks

Pointed toothpicks

Paper, glue, dish of water

A magnet

YOU DO:

1. Poke the tacks into one side of the cork.

2. Glue or push a paper sail onto a toothpick and poke it into the opposite side of the cork. You now have a miniature boat.

3. Fill a dish with water for your lake or ocean, prop it up on 2 blocks, and place the boat at one end.

4. Stand behind the boat and reach underneath the ocean with a magnet. Just move the magnet slowly under the boat and it will sail across the water like magic!

5. If you'd like a sturdier boat, use a block of balsa wood or a chunk of cork, a larger sail, and a few more tacks. Ask your hardware store if they sell magnetic strips to replace the tacks.

ADD-ONS:

What other kinds of boats can you make? Experiment with various containers for the hulls; paper or cloth of different shapes, sizes, and designs for the sails. Add a flag, a cabin, a wheel, and perhaps some tiny sailors.

Be a Boat Builder

Boating is one of the world's most popular sports. Ever since early man first used a log to float across a small stream and a raft to carry goods down a river, boats have been both useful and enjoyable.

When the explorers came to America, they found Native Americans paddling birchbark canoes. Pretend you are an Indian or an explorer and make a canoe, a raft, or a fleet of different kinds of boats.

YOU NEED:

Paper, cardboard, or real birchbark

Milk cartons, margarine containers

Balsa wood, popsicle sticks

Ice cream sticks, toothpicks

Scissors, crayons, felt markers

Clay or fun dough

YOU DO:

1. Cut and fold the cardboard or bark into a long canoe shape. Staple or glue the ends together.

2. Add cardboard seats and ice cream stick oars. Decorate your canoe to look like birchbark and add Indian symbols, if you wish. Rig up some pipe cleaner or clay people and put them in the boats. Will your canoe stay upright in your bathtub or wading pool, or in a nearby stream?

3. Try carving a simple boat shape out of balsa wood, or use a milk carton or other container for the hull. Add a paper sail on a toothpick or stick, and have a boat race.

4. Construct a simple raft out of some popsicle or other sticks. Hoist a square of cloth or paper for a sail, as Huckleberry Finn did, and a miniature bandana-lunch on a stick.

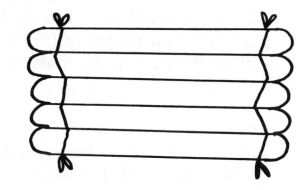

5. Put 3 popsicle sticks together. Make the middle stick longer than the other 2 by adding a pointed prow of clay or wood, or by trimming off 2 of the sticks. Now you have a South Pacific *catamaran*. You will find that it is hard to capsize this kind of boat. The more complicated version of a catamaran has twin hulls or bottoms.

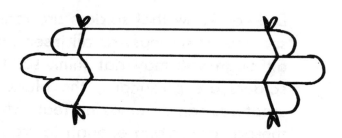

6. You might want to create a rowboat, a speedboat, a cruiser with a cabin, or a fleet of sailboats such as sloops, yawls, or schooners with one or many sails. Finally, complete your boat collection with a freighter and a giant ocean liner. Just use your imagination and whatever materials you can scrounge up.

7. To make an Indonesian *prau*, bend cardboard into a canoe shape, with both ends pointed up. Flatten out 1 side slightly and connect an outrigger, or floating spar, to the curved side. Place a triangular sail in the middle of the prau.

ADD-ONS:

Increase your boating knowledge by learning some of the jargon. Your friends will be impressed when you say *bow* (front) and *stern* (back); *forward* and *aft*; *port* (left) and *starboard* (right). Can you name the various parts of a boat, such as the jib sail, the main sail, the rudder, centerboard, keel, mast, cleat, and boom?

Read some boating books, or ask someone with a sailboat to teach you how to sail. You will want to know water safety and how to steer the boat and handle the sails to "catch the wind." An exciting moment is when the boat "comes about," and everyone has to shift to the opposite side! Do you think you could follow a course and run before the wind, tack, and jibe?

Spider Webs

Did you know that spiders are really not insects? They don't have three body-sections or six legs, as all insects must. Spiders are really very shy creatures, although you may not think so. Only two of the 50,000 different kinds of spiders are poisonous, the black widow and the brown recluse. These tiny creatures can do amazing feats when spinning a web. The delicate-looking silk threads are strong enough to trap much larger caterpillars and locusts. Here are some ways to make a spider web.

Crepe Paper Web

1. To make a giant black spider web, make alternate cuts through a package of black crepe paper (almost to the end). Unfold and you will have a giant web from which your spiders can hang.

2. To make smaller webs, fold several pieces of black crepe paper; then make alternate cuts and unfold; then pull apart the shreds. Your spider web will emerge.

Spiders To Make

1. A nifty way to make a spider is with a hair barrette and 4 rubber bands. Cut each one to make long rubber strips.

2. Decorate the barrette with black magic markers. Add red eyes.

3. Open the barrette and slide the rubber bands through for the legs; use another one as a hanger to suspend the spider from the web.

Thanks to Alexis Rubin for this idea.

String on Paper

1. Glue down string or yarn in a spider web design on a piece of construction paper or cardboard. Or arrange yarn on a piece of paper, then spray with blue or black paint.

2. When the paper dries, lift off the yarn and a spider web will appear.

3. Draw in a tiny spider or glue one on made of yarn.

String and Nails

1. Construct a web out of a board, nails (with large heads), and string or yarn. Hammer in the nails in a random design; then wind string in and out of the nails.

2. Dangle a spider (created from black paper and yarn or pipe cleaners) from the web. More complicated designs can be made with smaller nails and colored embroidery thread.

Real Spider Web

1. To capture a real spider web, go out in a field or into a barn in the early morning and look for a web.

2. When you discover one, place a sheet of construction paper behind it, and gently nudge it off onto the paper.

3. Cover the fragile web with plastic wrap. Frame your real spider web and hang it up, or display it in your nature corner.

ADD-ONS:

Think up other ways of making spiders large and small. Learn some spider songs or poems or make up your own. Read some spider web stories, like *Charlotte's Web.*

House of Cards

Have you ever tried building a house of cards? This building game, invented about the same time by two creative artists, Arnold Arnold and Charles Eames, is quite easy to make and will provide hours of challenging fun.

YOU NEED:

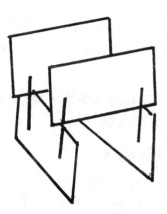

File or playing cards, or cardboard

Ruler, pencil

Scissors or X-Acto knife

Felt marking pens

YOU DO:

1. Measure and draw 2 lines at each top edge of some file or card-board cards.

2. Carefully cut along the slits. If using heavy cardboard or other thick material, make the slots a little wider than the thickness of the board, to prevent bending.

3. Insert one card into another by fitting the slots together. Enjoy creating houses, buildings, and other structures with your slotted cards. How high a house or tower can you build?

4. To make a free-standing house or box, cut longer slots (beyond the center) at right angles to the

sides. Then glue or tape on a top and a bottom, as in illustration.

5. You can also hook together paper tubes, cups, and plates by this slot method. Cut out and color scenery and props for a puppet show (a tree, bush, cottage, bench, bed, chair, table) using this kind of construction.

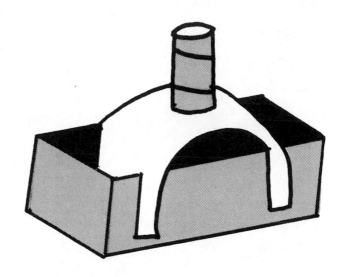

ADD-ONS:

Decorate the cards if you wish. A deck of playing cards will provide its own colorful decorations. If you want to build a semi-permanent street or city, you could draw in windows, doors, etc.

Younger children will do better with heavier cards of cardboard or colorful poster board.

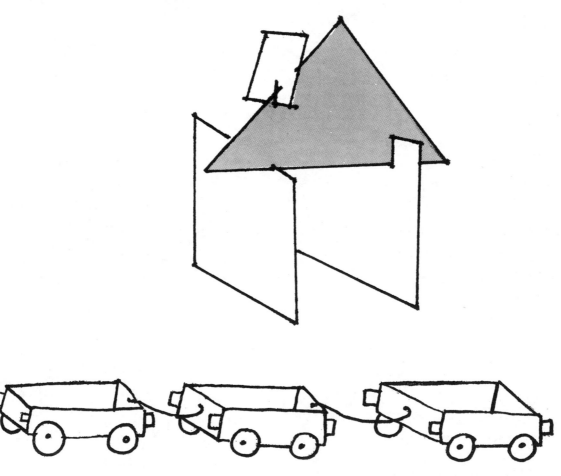

PASTES AND PUTTIES

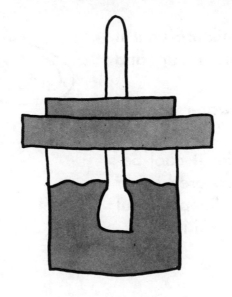

Thin Paste

YOU NEED:

- ¼ cup sugar
- ¼ cup flour
- ½ teaspoon powdered alum (available in drugstores)
- 1¾ cups water
- ¼ teaspoon oil of cinnamon

YOU DO:

1. Mix the sugar, flour, and alum in a pan.
2. Gradually add 1 cup of water, stirring vigorously.
3. Heat and stir the mixture until it boils and becomes clear and smooth.
4. Add the remaining water and the oil of cinnamon.
5. Stir the paste and let it cool before storing it in a covered jar or other container. Will keep without refrigeration for several months.

Library Paste

YOU NEED:

- ¼ cup cornstarch
- ¼ cup unflavored gelatin
- 1 cup water
- Oil of cloves
- Double boiler

YOU DO:

1. Mix the cornstarch and the warm water together in the top of a double boiler; then add the gelatin.

2. Stir over the heat until the mixture turns into a thin, smooth paste. Bring to a boil and continue cooking, stirring constantly, until the paste is the consistency of thick cream.

3. Add a few drops of oil of cloves to preserve the paste. Let cool and keep in a jar with a tight lid.

Cornstarch Paste

YOU NEED:

⅛ cup gum arabic (available in art or drug stores)

1 cup warm water

½ cup sugar

⅛ cup cornstarch

Boric acid

YOU DO:

1. In a pot, dissolve the gum arabic in the cup of warm water. Then add the sugar and the cornstarch and bring to a boil, stirring until the paste is the consistency of light cream.

2. Add a pinch of boric acid to keep the paste from becoming mildewed. Keep in a tightly covered jar.

Glutin Chips

YOU NEED:

Flour

Water

Muslin or cheesecloth

YOU DO:

1. Scoop a handful of flour onto a square of cheesecloth and wrap securely like a bag.

2. Place the bag under running water, kneading the flour as the water runs over it. When the water is no longer milky, most of the starch will be removed, with just glutin left.

3. Place the glutin in a glass dish or jar and let it dry. It can be kept without refrigeration for a long time.

4. When you need some paste, chip off flakes of the glutin and add a few drops of cold water. Let stand a few minutes, then knead until the mixture becomes soft and pliant. Add more water to thin out, if necessary.

Glue

Glue has been around longer than almost any other art material, besides natural dyes and paints used during prehistoric times. Ancient drawings in caves have been discovered that were painted with sticky plant juices, raw eggs, and dried blood mixed with coloring. Later on, glue was made by boiling animal bones and hides. In the early 20th century, artificial or synthetic substances such as resins and polymers were used to make glue.

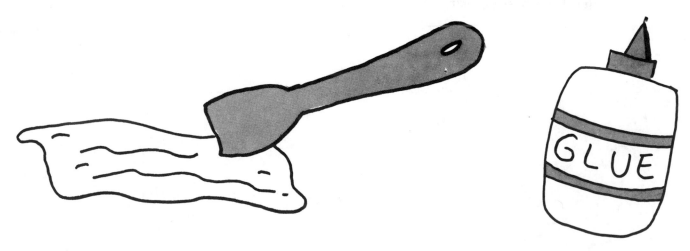

Transparent Glue

YOU NEED:

¼ cup unflavored gelatin

⅔ cup acetic acid (available at
   drug stores)

¾ cup water

Cold water

YOU DO:

1. Soak the gelatin in ¾ cup water for 12 hours; then heat up the mixture until the gelatin dissolves.

2. Stir in the acetic acid and add cold water to make 2 cups. This recipe makes a glue strong enough to cement glass. Dilute it with water when working with paper, mounting photos, etc.

3. You can also brush this glue over pictures for a protective coating. Wipe off any excess glue with a cloth or sponge soaked in warm water.

Casein Glue

YOU NEED:

1 cup skimmed milk

2 tablespoons white vinegar

2 tablespoons water

½ teaspoon baking soda

YOU DO:

1. Pour the skimmed milk and the vinegar into a pot and heat slowly. Stir until the mixture thickens and lumps form.

2. Remove from the stove and keep stirring as long as lumps or curds are forming.

3. Use a strainer to separate the curds from the liquid.

4. Put the sticky curds into a jar and add the water and baking soda. Watch what happens. The mixture will bubble and change into a gooey white glue, to be used like regular white school glue.

Flexible Forms

YOU NEED:

Clay

Clear or colored nail polish

YOU DO:

1. Make shapes out of clay (a ball, snake, heart).

2. Paint over the top and sides with clear or colored nail polish. Let dry and do this again several times until you have a soft, flexible "skin" that can serve as a mold for plaster of paris or as a doll hat, basket, heart shape, etc.

Rubber Cement Eraser

Did you know that you can make an eraser out of rubber cement? Pour a glob on a piece of waxed paper and let it dry. Then roll it into a ball. You will have a fine "pick up" eraser!

Toothpaste Putty

YOU NEED:

- 1 small tube of toothpaste
- 1 teaspoon white glue
- 2 teaspoons cornstarch
- ½ teaspoon water

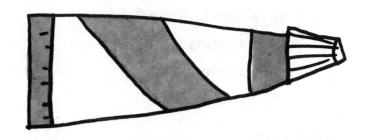

YOU DO:

1. Mix together the toothpaste, glue, and cornstarch.
2. Add the water and keep on mixing until a lump of putty forms.
3. Squeeze and roll the putty into a ball. Enjoy playing with your toothpaste putty for 10 or 15 minutes. When it gets too dry, soften it with a drop of water.
4. If you wish to save your creations, let them dry in the open air for about a day. They will be rock hard. Otherwise, store in a plastic bag or a jar with a lid.

Silly Putty

YOU NEED:

- 1 tablespoon liquid starch
- 2 tablespoons white glue
- Food coloring (optional)

YOU DO:

1. Put the starch and glue in a bowl and let it stand for about 5 minutes.
2. Add a few drops of food coloring, if you wish.
3. Mix well until the starch is absorbed and the color spreads evenly through the putty.
4. Store in a jar or a plastic bag (small plastic eggs make a perfect container) overnight before using.
5. Play with your silly putty by molding it, pulling it, bouncing it, and using it to pick up comic strip pictures (flatten a ball of putty and press it down on the newspaper).

Plastic Gel

YOU NEED:

1 envelope unflavored gelatin

3 tablespoons water

Food coloring

Plastic coffee can lid

YOU DO:

1. Stir the gelatin and water in a pot. Add a few drops of food coloring and cook over medium heat, stirring constantly until dissolved.

2. Remove from the heat and pour into a plastic coffee can lid or similar container. Push any bubbles that form to the edges.

3. Let harden for 1 or 2 days. Lift out and you will have a plastic-like material to cut into jewelry, discs, a guitar pick, or whatever you want.

ADD-ONS:

Make a variety of colors. Use marking pens to create designs. Cut out holiday and other shapes, poke a hole in the top and hang up as a decoration, sun-catcher, or on a string for chimes and mobiles. You can also make tiny doll dishes and other accessories.

MODELING COMPOUNDS

Papier Mâché Mash

Papier mâché crafts have been enjoyed by American children for many years and are a favorite activity of children in China, Japan, India, and Mexico. You can buy a mix at most art and hobby stores, but here is a basic one that's fun to make.

YOU NEED:

Newspaper, paper egg cartons, construction and tissue paper

Flour, water, paste, oil of cloves

YOU DO:

1. Tear and shred newspapers, paper egg cartons, or paper into small pieces. Soak the bits in warm water overnight.

2. Drain off the excess water and then squeeze the pulp through a strainer or your fingers.

3. Slowly mix some flour into a bowl of water until it is like heavy cream, and add a little paste (cornstarch or library). Add a few drops of oil of cloves.

4. Next, stir in the paper pulp. It should be quite thick. If used for a modeling compound, thin it with water.

Colorful Soap Dough

YOU NEED:

2 cups flour

½ cup salt

2 tablespoons liquid detergent

1 tablespoon liquid tempera paint

YOU DO:

1. Mix all of the ingredients together, adding a little water to make the dough pliable.
2. Make several batches of different colors.
3. Enjoy working with this smooth, fragrant dough.

Sand Dough

YOU NEED:

1 cup sand

½ cup cornstarch

1 tablespoon powdered alum

¾ cup hot water

Food coloring (optional)

YOU DO:

1. Mix the sand, cornstarch, and alum in a bowl.
2. Slowly add the hot water and stir vigorously.
3. Add some food coloring, if you wish.
4. Cook over medium heat until thick.
5. Let cool before using. Have fun molding into all kinds of objects. Let your finished projects dry in the sun for several days. Store unused sand-clay in an airtight container.

Note: This compound does not need shellac or varnish, since it dries to a grainy, stonelike consistency.

Dryer Lint Dough

Here's an unusual modeling compound to try. Use it as you would papier-mâché. It will be quite rough when dried, if shaped over an object; and smooth, if pressed into a mold. So start saving the lint from your dryer now, since it will probably take you quite a long time to save enough for a project! If you are too impatient, try concocting ⅓ of the recipe.

YOU NEED:

3 cups of dryer lint

2 cups water

⅔ cup flour

Oil of cloves

YOU DO:

1. Stir together the lint and water in a saucepan.
2. Add the flour, stirring to prevent lumps.
3. Shake in 2 or 3 drops oil of cloves.
4. Cook over low heat, stirring until the mixture forms peaks.
5. Pour out onto newspapers to cool.
6. Form the dough into a large ball, or shape with your hands over a ball, balloon, box, or cardboard tubes. Press the dough into molds of various sizes and shapes, or use like papier-mâché.

This unusual dough will take 3—5 days to dry thoroughly; when it does, it will be hard and quite durable.

See *Mudworks* by MaryAnne Kohl
for other fun modeling ideas

Sawdust Modeling Compound Relief Map

If you've ever been up in an airplane and looked down at the earth below, you've probably noticed that the hills and mountains look like small and large bumps. Everything is in miniature. You can make a relief map that looks like the earth as viewed from the sky just for fun or as part of a school project.

YOU NEED:

 2 cups sawdust

 ⅓ cup wallpaper paste

 1 cup water

 Cardboard, about 12 inches square

 Aluminum foil, tempera paint

YOU DO:

1. Mix the wallpaper paste, sawdust, and water with a stick or your hands to make a stiff clay.

2. Cover the cardboard with foil, and scoop out some sawdust clay onto the foil.

3. Mold the clay into hills and mountains, valleys, islands, and a river or lake.

4. Let your relief map dry for several hours or overnight. Then paint it in colors to look like water and land forms. Add small bits of green sponge, twigs, and pebbles, if you wish.

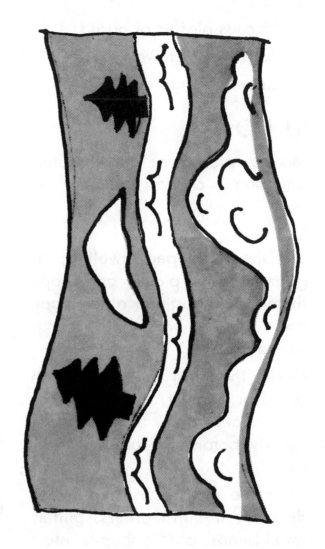

Plaster Ghosts, Angels, and Tunnel Shapes

Here's a nifty way to shape cloth into wild and weird shapes!

YOU NEED:

    1 cup water

    1½ tablespoons powdered
      alum

    1½ cups plaster of paris

    Cloth, paper towels, gauze

    Tempera paints

YOU DO:

1. Mix up plaster of paris, water, and alum in a large tin can or old bowl.

2. Quickly dip small pieces of cloth, old sheets, paper toweling, or gauze into the plaster and drape them over a bottle or other shape (milk carton, wire form, cardboard cone).

3. Model the form to look like an angel or a ghost, or a tunnel for your cars and trains. Work quickly before the plaster hardens.

4. After the plaster dries, paint or decorate it with markers, glitter, small beads, plastic shapes, etc.

Plaster of Paris Sculpture in a Bag

Here's an easy, fun way to enjoy plaster of paris without all the mess.

1. Just pour a few tablespoons of plaster of paris into a ziplock bag. Add some dry tempera paint and a little water (enough to form a soft dough).

2. Close the bag tightly, then use your hands to squeeze the plaster and water into a usable dough. It will start to get warm and harden almost immediately.

3. Pour immediately into a mold or onto waxed paper to shape; or form the dough into a shape right in the bag.

4. Stick in a paper clip before the plaster hardens, if you want to hang up your work. Leave out in the air for at least an hour, then remove your creations from the bag or mold, and paint, if you wish.

Soap Crayons

Soap is the perfect material for doing a simple sculpture. It's inexpensive and can be recycled in the bathtub when your carving is completed.

YOU NEED:

A bar of soft soap (Ivory, Dove, Camay are good)

Pointed stick, paper clip, potato peeler

Knife with a dull blade

Round toothpick, water color paints

YOU DO:

1. Choose soap that is soft enough to carve. Ivory floats, for a wonderful bathtub toy.

2. Make an outline of your sculpture with a pointed stick (a wooden orange stick is perfect), or just take your knife and start chipping away at the soap. Hold the bar of soap in one hand and *carefully* cut with the other. Always cut away from your body. (Some carvers brace their thumb against the soap as they cut or chip.)

3. Do a little bit at a time; mistakes are hard to repair; and so are cut fingers!

4. Square or rectangular sculptures are easier than round ones, but each of them will need the edges smoothed out after you have made the basic cuts. Keep turning the soap as you work, so your work will look good from all angles.

5. To create texture, use a popsicle or orangewood stick, paper clip, or potato peeler. When adding features (a big nose, tail, trunk, ears, etc.), use a

toothpick to join the small soap pieces to the sculpture. Fill in small holes or cracks with a paste made of soap shavings and water.

6. When your sculpture is finished, smooth it off by dipping it quickly in warm water and rubbing it with your fingers.

7. Color your carving or leave it plain. It will look a little like marble.

8. Display your soap sculptures on your treasures shelf or give them as a gift. Recycle any spare ones in your bathtub.

ADD-ONS:
Plaster of paris blocks also make good carving stones. Let the plaster harden in a cut-down milk carton. Then peel away the container.

Soft Soap Carving

Here's a nifty way to use up those leftover pieces of soap by recycling them into creative carvings.

YOU NEED:

    4 tablespoons soap scraps

    3 tablespoons water

    2 tablespoons crayon shavings

    Sculpting tools

YOU DO:

1. Chop the soap into tiny pieces and place in a pan with the water.

2. Cook over low heat, stirring until all of the water disappears.

3. Add the crayon shavings, and stir until they melt into the soap. Use similar colors, or just one, to keep them bright.

4. With a wooden spoon or spatula, scrape the mixture onto waxed paper and let it cool. Be sure to clean the pan and spoon immediately, unless you use disposable ones.

5. Press the mixture into rectangular or block shapes, or make small balls. Let your soapstones harden for several days.

6. Carve the soapstones with a dull knife, pointed stick, nail, or anything sharp, taking care not to hurt yourself.

ADD-ONS:

You can make boats, decorated guest bars, soap jewels, animals, holiday shapes . . . or whatever you can dream up. Wrap the completed creations in colorful paper and ribbons and give them as gifts.

Natural Clay Modeling

Playing with homemade clay or dough is fun and easy, but working with moist, natural clay is much more satisfying. Stoneware clay, in brown or gray, can be purchased in bulk at a hobby or art store. The natural clay, if stored properly, improves with time. (Did you know that Japanese potters keep special clay for years for their grandchildren to use?)

YOU NEED:

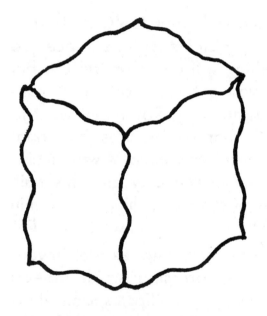

Natural clay

Tools (clay stick or nail stick, small blocks, rolling pin, hair pin, dull knife, etc.)

Extra water, sponge

Newspapers, plastic, or oilcloth

Wooden board or cardboard

Tempera or acrylic paint

Shellac, clear varnish, or colorless nail polish

YOU DO:

1. Work over a table covered with plastic, oilcloth, or newspapers. You could also use a piece of cardboard or wood as a clay board. Keep the extra clay moist by covering it with plastic or a damp cloth.

2. Soften the clay and work out the air bubbles by squeezing, pounding, rolling, and flattening it. Experiment with various shapes and techniques. Enjoy working the clay with your hands.

3. Form the clay into animals, bowls, figures, faces, or whatever you want. You could pinch a pot, or use the coil method. Then fill your pot or basket with small fruits and vegetables.

4. Wet your fingers and smooth out the clay, or use a damp sponge. Then let it dry a little before decorating with your tools. It's best to make objects of one piece, so nothing will crack or fall off, but as you get more adept at handling the clay, you might want to add a handle, features, hair, and/or other decorations. Always moisten the added clay and the main piece before attaching. Use a thin mixture of clay and water, or *slip*.

5. Create interesting textures in your clay by pressing small objects (shells, paper clips, spools, buttons, pencil eraser, small block, etc.) into the surface of the objects you make.

6. Large finished pieces should be scooped out inside so they won't be too heavy and will fire better in a kiln.

7. Let your completed creations dry for a few days. This "greenware" can be painted with tempera or acrylic paints.

Wedging: Older children should learn how to "wedge" the clay (cutting moist clay in pieces, then throwing it down on a board to get rid of air bubbles) before making something. Real potters use a special wedging board or box with an attached wire, before beginning a project. They cut a lump of clay in half, and rejoin the halves by turning, pounding, and squeezing the clay against the board. The process is repeated several times.

Storing Clay: Natural or ceramic clay will last a long time, if you store it properly. A garbage can and two plastic bags are best for keeping large quantities moist, but just a tightly sealed plastic bag will do. Form leftover clay into small balls, hollow out a hole with your thumb, and put in a little water before covering. If the clay dries out, hammer it into little bits, then soak it in water to restore it to a workable consistency.

Firing the Clay: It's best to take clay objects to a commercial kiln to be fired. Before firing, let the pottery dry well for several days. If you were careful to wedge the clay first, added the parts correctly with slip, and made your walls thick enough, the firing should be successful. A color glaze added after the first firing will make your pottery even more beautiful. There are several products on the market now that can be boiled or baked and turn out looking like porcelain, bisque, or real ceramics.

Ceramic Clay Tiles

YOU NEED:

Low-fire red clay or ceramic clay

Objects from nature: leaves, weeds, flowers, reeds, pine needles

Sheet of acetate, rolling pin, knife

2 strips of wood, about 18" long and ½" thick

Cardboard, aluminum foil

Ruler, tempera paint, or glaze

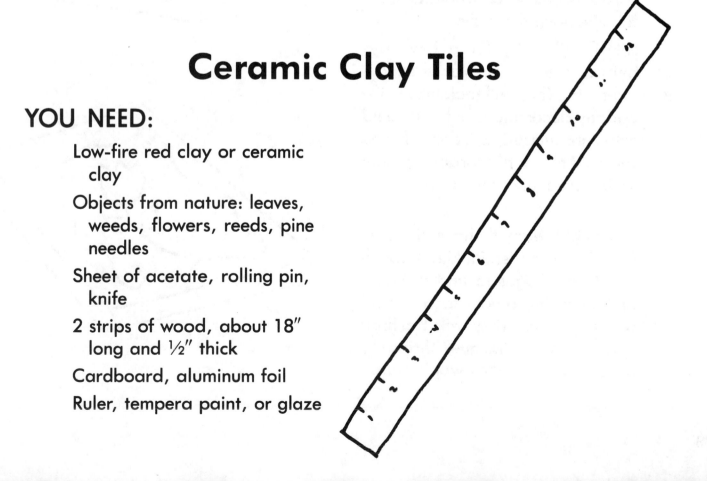

YOU DO:

1. Form the clay into a large lump and wedge it by throwing it down on the clay board or table a few times to remove the air bubbles.

2. Place the 2 sticks down on the table about 6 to 8 inches apart as guidelines; then roll out the clay into a flat slab.

3. Arrange leaves, weeds, flowers, or whatever you have gathered, on top of the slab, leaving room for a border. Place the acetate sheet over the arrangement and press the leaves into the clay with the rolling pin.

4. Use a ruler with a straight edge to help you cut the slab into a square or a rectangle.

5. Carefully lift off the tile (a spatula helps) and let it dry on a piece of cardboard covered with aluminum foil. Remove the leaves.

6. Let the tiles dry for a few days before painting and/or shellacking them. They will look nice without any decoration, but you could add an incised border, if you want. And don't forget to sign your name and the date on the back.

7. You might want to have the tiles fired in a commercial kiln. Look in the Yellow Pages to find a place, or take them to your local school or craft shop. They will be fired twice, first a "bisque" firing to harden them so they won't break,

then a second firing after you glaze them. Use colored glaze to outline the nature shapes, or to make a border.

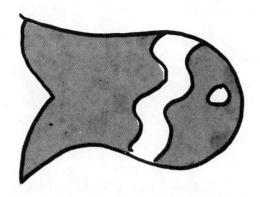

ADD-ONS:

You can make all kinds of interesting tiles this way: name or number tiles, pictures, or imprinted items made with coins, shells, and so forth. Try doing a hand print or a thumb drawing.

Divide the slab into 4 parts, and make small tiles or coasters.

To hang your finished tiles, press a paper clip into the back while the clay is still fairly soft, or use a gummed hanger after the tile has hardened.

DYEING, SEWING, AND WEAVING

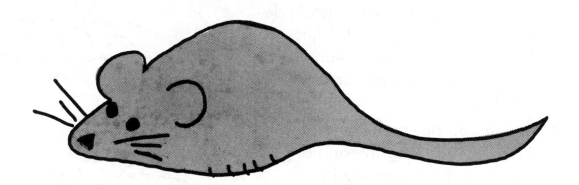

Japanese Shibori Designs

Shibori is an ancient Japanese method of dyeing cloth, after making patterns or designs in it by stitching, clamping, wrapping, or pleating the material.

YOU NEED:

Unbleached muslin

Fabric dyes (packaged or natural)

Needle and nylon thread

Scissors, pencil

Rubber gloves, stick, or tongs

YOU DO:

1. Cut the muslin to the size you want. To create a wood grain design, draw 5 horizontal lines on the fabric, and sew along each line with tiny stitches or a sewing machine.

2. When you get to the end of each line, leave a long thread hanging down, without knotting it.

3. Stitch all 5 lines in this way, leaving a length of unknotted thread at the end of each.

4. Next, pull the threads until the fabric gathers up tightly. Then securely knot the thread with a double knot. (You may have to ask for help at this point.)

5. Have an adult put the fabric into the dye bath (follow directions on the package). It's a good idea to wear rubber gloves, or use tongs or a stick, when handling the dyed fabric.

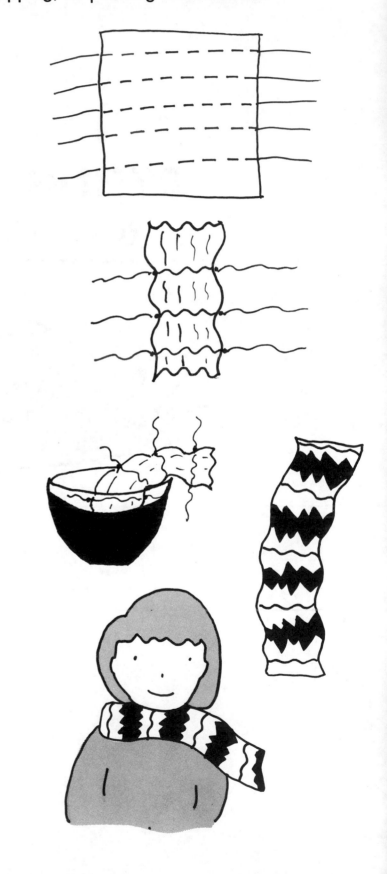

6. After the dye takes, rinse the cloth thoroughly in cold water until the water runs clean.

7. Cut the threads and straighten out the fabric. You now have a beautiful Shibori design. How will you use your dyed fabric? For a scarf, a purse, a placemat or napkin, a doll dress?

8. To make other patterns, use the same method of dyeing, but vary the sewing design as follows:

   To create a pine cone design, draw horizontal lines about 4 inches apart. Fold the fabric on each line and make small stitches around the 12 semi circles.

   Leave a length of thread at the end of each one. Pull the thread to gather the fabric, knotting each one, as before.

   For a fold-and-stitch pattern, draw 5 winding, diagonal lines, as in illustration, and proceed as before.

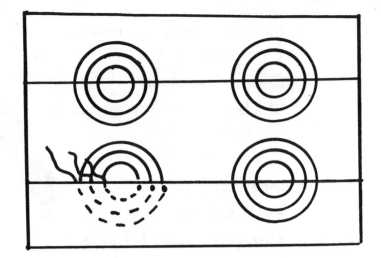

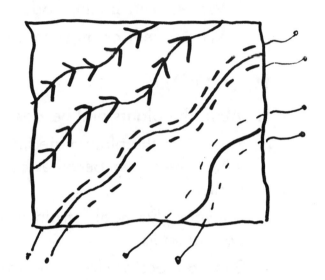

ADD-ONS:

Sew and dye several pieces of cloth of the same pattern and put them together to make a table runner, dresser scarf, wall hanging, tunic, or whatever appeals to you. Mix and match the designs, too.

Native American Natural Dyes

Native Americans used plants for dyeing wool, cotton, and other fibers. The dyes produced beautiful, soft colors. You can make natural dyes by experimenting with plants, flowers, berries, and seeds.

YOU NEED:

Sunflower seeds or larkspur petals to make blue

Grapes for black

Blueberries or raspberries for purple

Walnut shells for brown

Moss for green

Beets for red

Marigold petals for yellow

Water, salt, baking soda

White sheet or other fabric

YOU DO:

1. Wash the plants and berries and pound any that are hard.

2. Place 1 of the plant materials into a small pot of water and bring to a boil. When the water becomes colored (longer for deeper colors), remove from heat.

3. Let your dye cool, strain it into a bowl or jar, and add a little salt and baking soda.

4. Soak a piece of cloth in warm, clear water and place it in the dye bath. Let it soak for several hours.

5. Then remove it and rinse well in cold water until no more color runs out.

6. Hang your lovely, naturally dyed cloth up to dry, away from direct sunlight or heat.

7. How many different colors can you make? Which plant material seems to work the best? Were you surprised at the colors?

ADD-ONS:

Make a hanky or a scarf out of your dyed cloth. Sew some doll clothes or a belt or headband, or whatever you want to create.

Turn hard-boiled eggs into warm, soft-colored Easter eggs with natural dyes.

Sunshine Dyes

While your outdoor dyeing area is set up, try experimenting with sun dyes.

1. Pick up several batches of sun dyes at your craft or hobby store, along with a jar of resist.

2. Use untreated cotton material to make wearable art (a shirt, bandana, draw-string purse, hat), as well as a picnic cloth, or a banner for your art fair or other neighborhood events.

3. Squeeze the resist out of a plastic bottle or apply it with a paintbrush to make your design. Then brush the dyes over the surface. Be really inventive and use several bright colors.

4. Leave the cloth out in the sun for about half an hour; watch what happens. The colors will gradually emerge in the sunlight, except where you put the resist.

5. Wash the cloth in warm, soapy water, and let it dry. Iron it, if you want a smooth look. What other projects can you think up to do with sunshine dyes?

Tie-and-Fade-Dyeing

Make T-shirts, placemats, napkins, scarves, and wall hangings by tying, removing, and adding color to plain fabric which doesn't have a permanent finish.

1. To create faded designs, you will use dark cotton material and soak it in a solution of half water and half chlorine bleach. Blue jean material requires a weaker solution.

2. Experiment with various ways of folding and tying the fabric: for stripes, accordion pleat it first, then tie in several places with string or rubber bands. Strips of plastic bags will create even wider stripes.

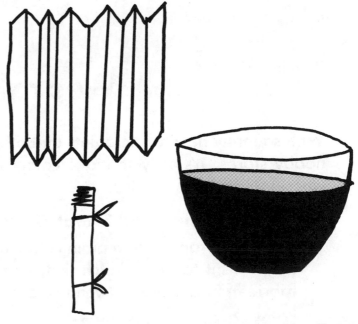

3. To make a large sunburst, hold the cloth in the center, let it hang down, and tie several times. For smaller circles, bunch the cloth up in a few spots and tie securely. (In Nigeria, they tie the cloth over and around a long stick to create their striking dyed material.)

4. Next, dip the tied fabric into the bleach solution for a few minutes (use a stick or rubber gloves). Remove from the bleach, cut the ties, and take a look at the unfolding design!

5. Rinse the T-shirt or placemat in cold water and hang it on a rack or clothesline to dry in the sunshine (this is an excellent outdoor activity), or in a clothes dryer.

6. Finally, iron out the wrinkles and put on your new "faded" fashion, or wrap it up for a gift.

7. Follow the same procedure with light-colored fabric and colorful dyes. Think up various combinations and patterns.

Wearable Art

With so many new fabric paints and other materials now available at craft and hobby stores, it's easy to make colorful works of art that will withstand many washings.

Decorated T-Shirts and Sweat Shirts

1. Choose cotton shirts in plain colors and jazz them up with fabric paints. You might want to do a sketch first, or try out the paints on a small part of the fabric first. Let dry between colors, unless you want a smeared or blended look.

2. To set the colors, put the shirts in a dryer for about 45 minutes on delicate. Wash in cold water with a mild detergent.

3. Sew on buttons, beads, and other bangles. Use velcro tabs for removable decorations. Sign your name to your work of art.

Pants, Jeans, Jackets, Scarves, and Tennis Shoes

1. Follow the directions above. You may want to just do the pockets, or embroider designs on the jeans and jackets.

2. Free-form painting on scarves and tennis shoes is just the thing!

Stitchery

Hand sewing can be a challenging but very useful project. Think of all of the things you could make. After a little practice, you will be sewing like a pro.

YOU NEED:

Scraps of colorful fabric

Needle and thread (nylon and embroidery)

Pins, scissors, embroidery hoop (optional)

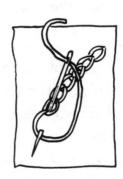

chain stitch

YOU DO:

The Basics

1. First learn how to thread a needle and roll a knot at the end of the thread.

2. Then practice the basic sewing stitches on a piece of burlap or cotton. They are:

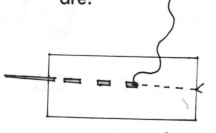

running stitch

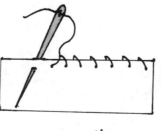

overcasting

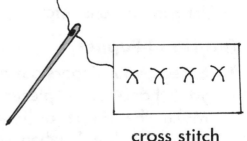

cross stitch

Toy Bag

1. Cut out 2 rectangles of fabric, or fold a long piece in half.

2. Turn the material inside out (top sides facing in) and pin the edges together, leaving about ½″ on each top side and the top edges open. Fold the two flaps down, and sew each one with the running stitch, to make an opening for the string. Then sew each side together and knot securely.

3. Turn the bag right side out and thread a colorful ribbon or string through the top (use a safety or bobby pin for easier threading). Sew or appliqué on a design and your draw-string bag will be ready to be filled with small toys, cards, jacks and a ball, or whatever use you can think up.

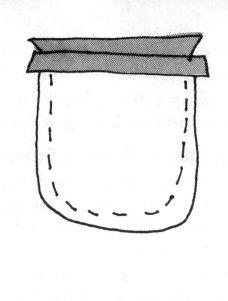

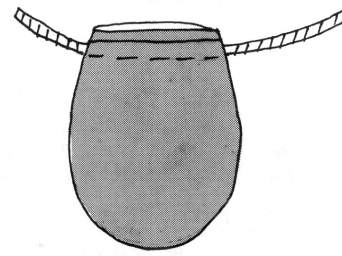

Stuffed Animals

1. Draw and cut out fabric for a doll or stuffed animal. Then follow the same general directions as above to sew your toy.

2. Leave a small section open so you can push in some stuffing material. Then sew it tightly closed, using an overcasting stitch.

3. Embroider on eyes, nose, mouth, and so forth before stuffing, if you wish. Sew or glue on felt scraps, buttons, etc.

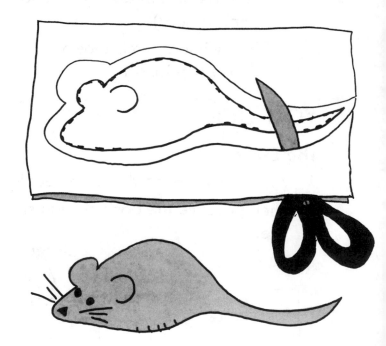

Felt Hand Puppet

1. Spread your fingers out and trace your hand on 2 pieces of felt. Make the shape a little bigger than your hand, when you cut it out. (See illustration.)

2. Using the running stitch, sew all of the edges together, except the bottom.

3. Turn the puppet right side out and add features with a felt marking pen, or by sewing, embroidering, or gluing on bits of fabric, buttons, beads, etc. Add a hat, pocket, collar . . .

4. Place your hand inside the puppet, with thumb and little finger stretched out, and make your puppet move and talk.

Doll Clothes

1. Design, cut out, and sew clothes and accessories for your animals and dolls out of colorful fabric scraps.

2. Add buttons, pockets, hankies, ties, belts, hats, etc.

3. If you are really ambitious, you can try making clothes for yourself too!

Weaving

Weaving Facts

Weaving is intertwining threads on a loom to make a fabric. The *warp* is a set of vertical threads stretched tightly and evenly across a frame. The *weft* thread is woven over and under the warp, alternating with each row.

Patterns are created by using different sizes, colors, and textures of weft threads such as yarn, ribbon, string, grasses, raffia, and other materials.

Here is an inexpensive and lightweight loom that you can put together and carry around with you.

YOU NEED:

A large styrofoam food tray or heavy cardboard

Thick yarn and other weaving materials

Bobby pin, ruler, pencil, scissors

Glue, masking tape

YOU DO:

1. Cut off the edges of the tray and measure ½" down from the top side in 2 places. Then draw a line across the tray, and mark off points or small lines, ¼" apart, stopping ½" from the right side. (See illustration.) There should be an uneven number of marks.

2. Do the same thing with the bottom of the tray. Next, carefully cut along all of the lines with a scissors or an X-Acto knife.

3. Your loom is now ready to be strung with the warp yarn. Thread the yarn or string in and out of the notches (leave 3" at each end) and secure the ends along the notches in the sides, as in illustration.

4. Take one of the cut-off side pieces of styrofoam and use it for a *shed stick*. Insert the stick through the warp threads at the bottom by weaving it in and out. When you turn the stick on its side, it will raise every other warp thread, making it easy to push or pull the yarn through.

5. Take a long piece of weaving yarn and thread it through the end of the bobby pin for a *needle*. Wrap tape around the open ends and you're ready to start weaving. Attach the end of the yarn to the left string at the top right of your loom, leaving about 3" of yarn.

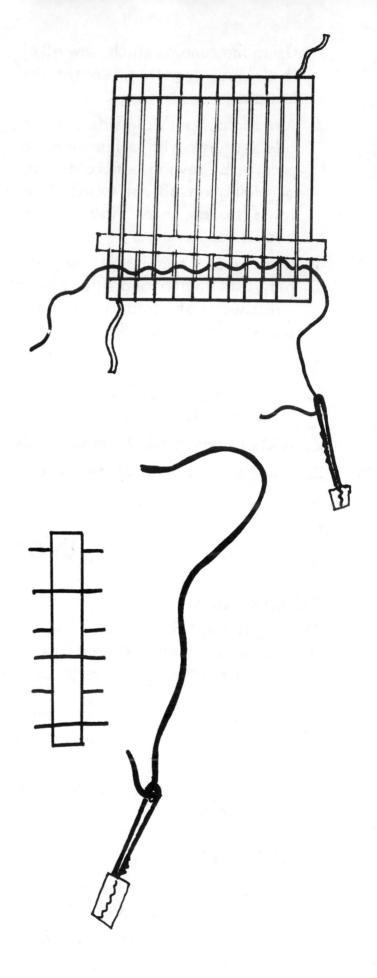

6. Weave in and out of the warp for the first row. Push it tight against the top with the flattened shed stick. Then put the stick on its side to pull up the warp, and push the needle through to the end. Continue this way weaving in and out on the way over; and on the way back, adjusting the stick and pushing the needle all the way through.

7. Tie on new yarn when you need it, varying the color, texture, and amount, if you wish. Watch your pattern emerge.

8. As you approach the bottom, remove the stick. Then cut the thread at the end of the last line, leaving a 3" tail. Knot the tail around the last warp thread and trim the end.

9. Pull the warp threads out from the top and bottom notches; then tie them together, 2 at a time, at both ends, making a fringe.

10. Leave your weaving as is for a small rug, doll blanket, or dresser scarf. For a wall hanging, cut off the top fringe above the knots, except for the one on each side, and turn the weaving over.

11. Lay a pencil or a dowel across the top, about 1" down, and brush on a thick line of glue just under the pencil. Next, wrap the top of the weaving around the pencil and press down so the material sticks together. (You

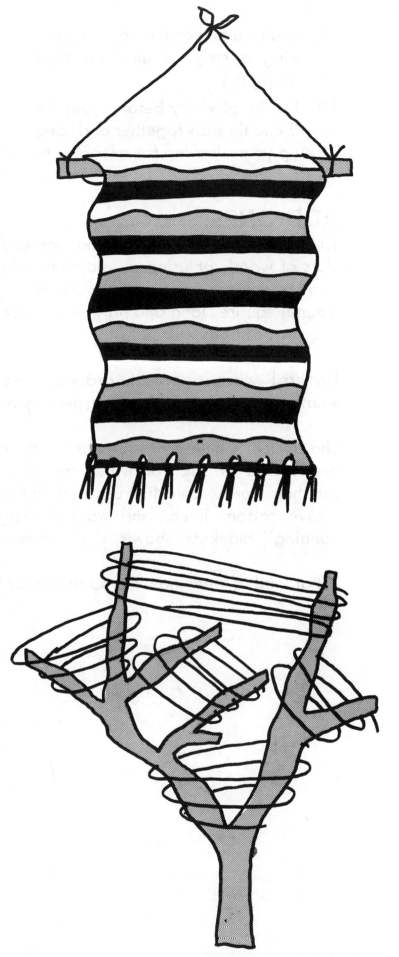

could reinforce the edge by running a strip of masking tape along it.)

12. Let the glue dry before tying the 2 end threads together and hang up your weaving for everyone to admire!

ADD-ONS:

There are many other looms that you could make, including nailing together 4 slats of wood, or using an old picture frame with rows of nails along the top and bottom, for stringing the warp; cutting slots in various shapes of cardboard (round, square, long and narrow, etc.) or more complicated large looms found in craft or hobby stores.

Natural weavings with grasses, reeds, dried weeds, foil, flowers, and whatever you can gather are especially nice. Try using a branch for your loom!

The ancient Chinese are famous for their beautiful woven silk tapestries; they even raised the silk worms that spun the thread. Native Americans are known for their sturdy, colorful rugs and clothing. Ancient Egyptians used looms to weave cotton, linen, and wool clothing. Modern artists weave large wall hangings, blankets, shawls, skirts, sweaters, belts, and other artistic items.

What kind of weaving will you tackle for your next project?

PHOTOGRAPHY AND OPTICS

From a box pinhole camera to a Stretch 35, photography has come a long way. The very first camera was invented in the 18th century (although it was described seven centuries earlier in Alhazen's *Book of Optics*) by two French men, Joseph Niepce, a physicist, and Louis Daguerre, a painter. The result was the *camera obscura,* a dark box with a tiny hole to let in light.

In 1989 Kodak came out with a disposable 35 mm camera that takes wide-angle color pictures. For a relatively small sum, you can shoot 12 landscape scenes or get your entire family or classroom into one 3½″ × 10″ photo! After you have taken the pictures, you just drop off the camera and buy another one. Also new is a 24-exposure throw-away "weekend" camera that even takes underwater shots.

Make a Pinhole Camera

Taking pictures with a store-bought camera is really fun, but using one you have made yourself is a little like magic!

YOU NEED:

Box with a tight lid

Black tempera paint or
construction paper

Heavy-duty aluminum foil

Cardboard, masking tape

Scissors, glue, pin

Photographic paper (from a
camera shop)

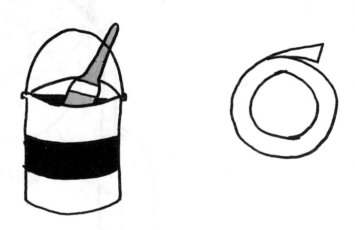

YOU DO:

1. Paint the inside of your box black, or cut and glue down black construction paper.

2. Next, cut a small hole, about 1″ square, in the center of the lid.

3. Cut a piece of foil slightly larger than the square and glue it between 2 cardboard frames.

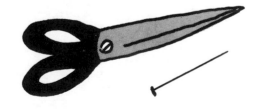

4. Tape the frame over the opening in the lid and poke a tiny hole with a pin in the center of the foil. Turn the pin to be sure you make smooth edges.

5. For a shutter, tape a flap of cardboard over the hole.

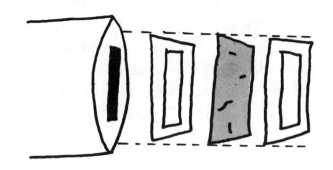

6. Finally, make a ring of masking tape and press it down inside the cover opposite the hole. The sticky tape will hold your photo paper in place.

7. Now you are ready to load your pinhole camera with "film." Find a dark place with a safe light (a yellow bulb or a flashlight covered with yellow cellophane) and open up the package of photo paper.

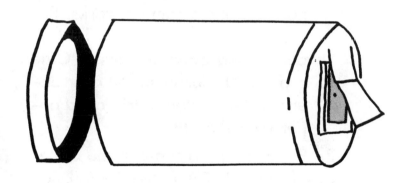

8. Cut the paper to size (about 4" × 5") and secure it, shiny side up, onto the tape inside the camera. Put on the lid and go out into the sunshine ready to take a picture.

9. With your back to the sun, point the camera, with the pinhole in front, at the object or person you want to photograph. Keep the camera very still as you lift up the flap. Hold it open for 1½ to 2 minutes. If you want to steady the camera on something (a table, stool, tree stump), that might even be better. Be sure your subject doesn't wiggle, either.

10. After taking the picture, go back under your safe light and remove the photo paper. Slip it

into an envelope and take it to your camera store to be developed and printed; or, even better, set up a darkroom and develop it yourself!

If you want to make a pinhole camera that uses an Instamatic film cartridge, consult the *Boy Scout Photography Manual*.

Nighttime Experiment

1. Here is a quick way to find out how a pinhole camera works. Remove both the top and the bottom of a round oatmeal carton. Glue a piece of aluminum foil over one end of the carton, and waxed paper over the other.

2. Punch a tiny pinhole in the center of the foil. Then hold the foil side next to a bare lightbulb and move it back and forth to "focus" it. What do you see on the waxed paper? An image will appear.

3. What would happen if you made the hole larger? The image would become blurred from too much light entering the box. Have you ever taken blurred pictures with a real camera? That probably happened because you moved the camera or focused incorrectly.

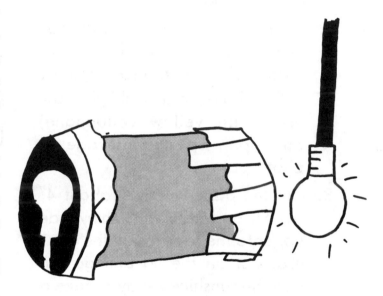

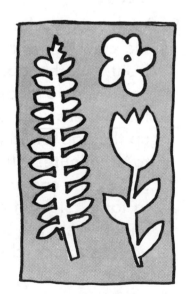

Sun Pictures

1. Here's a way of taking pictures outdoors without any camera at all. Buy a package of blueprint paper at a camera or hobby store.

2. Open it in a darkish place, away from the light, and place a sheet on a piece of cardboard or inside a box lid.

3. Tape several objects (from nature or around the house) on the paper, or cover them with clear plastic or a piece of glass.

4. Next, take your box lid outside in the sunshine for a few minutes. Then hurry back indoors. What did you and the sun create? Are you pleased with the design? If not, try again with another piece of blueprint paper.

5. To make the pictures permanent, fix them by dipping each one into a 3% hydrogen peroxide solution, or ¼ cup dissolved in 2 cups of water.

6. Rinse the picture off in cool water and blot it between paper towels. Frame your sun pictures or put them in a photo album or scrapbook.

Chalkboard Photography

Do you ever wish you could save a chalkboard drawing? Well, here's a nifty way to do that.

YOU NEED:

Chalkboard and chalk
Camera, film
Poster board
Construction paper, markers
Scissors

YOU DO:

1. Draw a picture on the board; then get your camera and take a photograph of it. You'll probably have to use flash, unless your chalkboard is outside.

2. Shoot as close up as you can, as the photo will come out lighter than the drawing, and you don't want it to be too small and far away.

3. After your film is processed, glue the photograph(s) to a piece of cardboard. Then write some appropriate comments underneath.

4. If you take a really good snapshot, have it enlarged, cut out a construction paper frame (decorate it, if you wish) and hang it in your room. This would also make a thoughtful gift.

Make a Viewfinder

YOU NEED:

Drawing paper, 8½" × 11"
Cardboard
Ruler, pencil, scissors

YOU DO:

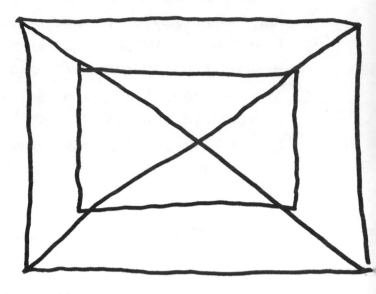

1. Cut a piece of cardboard the same size as your paper.

2. Measure and draw 2 straight diagonal lines to connect the corners of the cardboard rectangle. Next, draw and cut out a small rectangle in the center, where the 2 lines cross. Be sure the edges are straight. Now you have 2 rectangles, one the shape of the paper, and the other, the cut-out area.

3. This will be your viewfinder. Hold it up, close one eye and look through the opening at an object or a scene that you want to draw. Move the viewfinder back and forth until the object (a table, chair, vase of flowers) is touching the edge of the opening in at least 2 places.

4. Look at one of the small spaces around the vase. Does it look like a shape too? This space, called negative space, is as important as the vase itself when you are drawing your picture.

5. Now, begin your drawing. Instead of trying to draw the outlines of the vase and flowers, draw the

negative spaces, one at a time, starting with the outside ones first, then the inside ones. You'll be surprised at what a good vase of flowers you can draw.

6. Find other objects to draw using your viewfinder. The more you practice thinking and drawing like this, the easier it will become. Color your drawings, if you wish.

ADD-ONS:

Instead of a cardboard viewfinder, you could just use your hands. Hold a pencil in your right hand to make a vertical edge and keep the fingers of your left hand straight up. Stretch your thumb across so it touches your right thumb, and look through the opening you have made.

Rose-Colored Glasses

Make your world become more colorful with these unusual lorgnettes or glasses.

1. Glue colored cellophane into 2 plastic rings from a 6-pack holder. Attach a popsicle stick handle.

2. Cut an egg carton in half lengthwise; then cut circles in the sections and glue in pieces of colored cellophane. Attach a stick, decorate your fancy glasses, and view your world.

3. Make a cardboard lorgnette. Cut large eyeholes and glue in cellophane. Decorate it with markers, sequins, colored beads, etc. and you'll be all set for an opera or a masquerade party.

Giant Kaleidoscope

What fun to look through this kaleidoscope and see the beautiful colors and shapes swirl about and change before your very eyes!

YOU NEED:

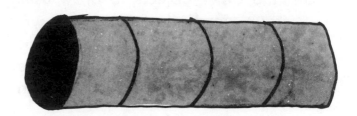

- 2 round cardboard cartons (oatmeal, cornmeal, grits) or a sturdy mailing tube
- Sheet of mylar or aluminum foil
- Construction paper, colored cellophane, shiny paper sequins, stickers, yarn, glitter
- Clear contact paper or acetate
- Tape, glue, scissors, markers
- Hat pin or long straight pin with head

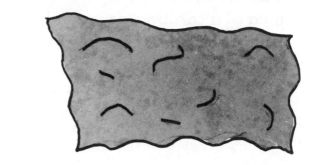

YOU DO:

1. Remove the tops and cut the bottoms off the round cartons. Then tape them together to make a long telescope. Or, cut the mailing tube to size.

2. Decorate the outside with construction paper, stickers, shiny paper shapes, etc.

3. Measure and cut mylar, foil, or other reflective material to fit the long tube and glue it inside, shiny side out. Use as little glue as possible.

4. Next, cut out 2 circles (about 9" in diameter, or ⅓ wider than the tube measures across), from the

unpeeled contact paper. Acetate with glued-down designs will make sturdier circles or disks.

5. Unpeel the backing from one of the circles and place it, sticky side up, on a work area. Then press on colorful cellophane shapes, stickers, sequins, yarn pieces, and so forth, to make exciting designs.

6. Take the backing off the second circle and press the sticky side down against your design to seal it. Reinforce the edges with tape, if you wish. Make several disks for even more fun.

7. Stick a long pin through the center of your disk and then through the rim of the tube. The disk will pivot around the pin.

8. Now, look through the other end of your giant kaleidoscope, spin the disk, and see what you have created!

ADD-ONS:
Another idea for a disk is to cut out the center of the cardboard lid on the carton, leaving about a ½" rim, and glue a decorated contact paper or acetate circle inside. Turn the lid slowly to see your design change.

Triple Disk Kaleidoscope

Older children will enjoy creating this elaborate triangular kaleidoscope.

YOU NEED:

    3 heavy cardboard rectangles
       about 3" × 12"

Mylar or aluminum foil

Heavy duty masking tape

Clear contact paper or acetate

Colored cellophane, sequins, glitter, stickers, yarn

3 metal poultry skewers or thin wooden shish-kebab skewers, or 7" length of stiff, straight wire

Small cardboard box or triangular wooden block

YOU DO:

1. Glue mylar or aluminum foil to the 3 cardboard rectangles.

2. Tape the rectangles together and fold them into a long triangular tube with the mylar or foil on the inside. Tape securely.

3. Decorate the outside of the tube to suit your fancy.

4. Make 3 colorful disks about 6" in diameter from the contact paper or mylar, just as you did for the Giant Kaleidoscope.

5. Balance the triangular tube on the wooden block so that one end is raised above the surface of the table, or cut down a small box to make a kaleidoscope stand. This way your disks will rotate without bumping the table.

6. Stick each disk onto a skewer, or cut the wire into 1½", 2", and 3" lengths and stick a disk onto each one.

7. Push the free end of each skewer or wire deeply into 1 corner of the triangular tube. One disk should

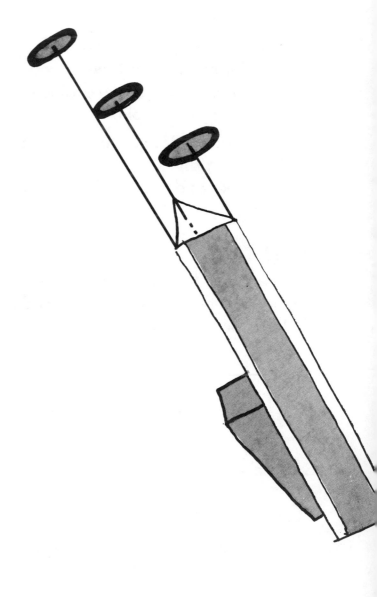

be positioned close to the tube, 1 in the middle, and 1 furthest from the tube on the longest wire.

8. Now sight down the kaleidoscope as you twirl each disk in turn or all together. Watch the wonderful display you have created.

Optical Illusions

There is a saying that seeing is believing. But you can't really believe in *everything* you see. Optical illusions happen when you look at certain lines and objects, and things begin to appear and disappear and to change. Lines move, objects of the very same size look different. Try these optical illusions, and experience some "magic."

1. Stare at a bright red object (a ball, a balloon, a circle). Then look at a white wall or piece of paper. What happens? You will see a *green* object. Green is the opposite of red on the color wheel. Now stare hard again at the red object; then close your eyes. Do you see a green circle?

2. Look at a pattern like this one. Do you see small gray dots at the corners?

   Stare at these flowers. Which circle looks larger? (The black one.) Measure them and you will see that they are both the same size!

   Draw a field of flowers, tracing around a coin for the centers. Which ones look larger now? Which one looks the smallest of all?

Which line looks longer? (The bottom one, but the lines are really the *same* size.) Does the top hat look taller than the brim, and the sail higher than the width of the boat? (Yes.) Measure them and you will see that all 4 lines are really the same length. This is called "geometrical contrast" illusion.

3. Stare hard at the monster's eyes. Do they begin to spin? Look closely at the kites flying above. Are they flat kites or box kites? Lines can trick us.

4. The "trident trick" is one of the oldest of all. Does this rake or trident have 2 prongs or 3? Cover the top half and see. This is an "impossible object" illusion.

5. Cut out 2 identical *curved* shapes and place them side by side. Which one looks longer? Now face them towards each other and they will look the *same* size. The same thing happens when you draw a landscape picture. Trees, houses, or telephone poles that are closer to the horizon line look smaller.

6. Make a construction paper landscape by cutting out shapes for grass, sky, houses, trees, bushes, etc. Put the objects in various parts of your scene. Does their size seem to change depending upon where they are? Where do they look the largest? Where the same size?

74

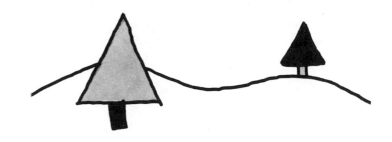

7. Draw some flowers, kites, balloons, fruits, and vegetables of different colors. Stare at each one for awhile, then look at a white piece of paper or a white wall. Do you see opposite colors? Cut out colored cellophane shapes and change the colors by putting one on top of another. How do the colors change? Can you see that red and blue make purple, yellow and blue make green, and yellow and red, orange? What do red and purple make?

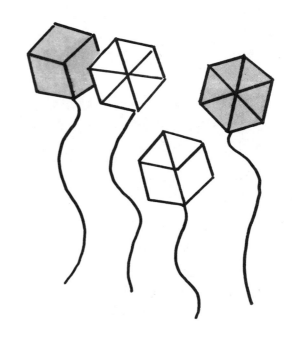

8. Upside-down faces are lots of fun to draw. Make an oval and put in the eyes, nose, mouth, and ears. Then add lines in the forehead and under the eyes. Put some hair on top, and a beard, or a bow or collar and tie, under the chin. Turn your paper upside down and you will see another face! Can you see faces in the trees or in the clouds? How about a man in the moon?

9. Make up your own optical illusion. Take the curved shapes you made and color designs on them. Do they look like people now? Lay them in a horizontal position. Do they turn into worms or snakes?

KITCHEN CHEMISTRY

Conduct these science experiments in your own kitchen.

Magic Pennies

Place a few old, dark pennies in a dish and sprinkle some salt on them. Then add a few drops of vinegar. Your pennies will sparkle and shine like new!

Vanishing Acts

Ask an adult to put a tablespoon of dry bleach powder in a glass. Then fill the bottom of another glass with water and add a few drops of red food coloring. Pour the red liquid into the first glass. What happens? The color will vanish like magic.

Hidden Colors

YOU NEED:

A glass with ½" of water in it

1 section of paper towel, cut in 1" wide strips

Markers

YOU DO:

1. Put a dot of black 2" from the bottom of 1 strip.
2. Place this end in the glass of water and the other over the rim.
3. Watch and see what happens. As the water races up the strip, dyes of different colors will appear to be going up the paper at various speeds.

4. Try other colors of ink and see what happens. Experiment with fruit and vegetable juices too.
5. Scientists call this chromatography.

Changing Colors

1. Shred up a handful of cabbage leaves.
2. Boil a cup of water in an enamel pot and carefully place the shredded cabbage in the pot. Cook for a few minutes. Turn off heat. Crush the leaves with a wooden spoon.
3. Wait an hour or so—the liquid turns purple!
4. Pour 2 tablespoons of purple water into each of several small glasses.
5. Then put a few drops of vinegar into 1 glass. The water will turn a rosy red.
6. Add ¼ teaspoon of baking soda to another glass. The color will change again, this time to green.
7. Try a little soap powder in a third glass, some lemon juice in a fourth. Substances that change the cabbage water to red are acids. Those that turn it green we call bases. We call the cabbage juice an indicator because it indicates, or shows, whether one substance or another is an acid or a base.

Flower Petals

Flower petals are also indicators. Try petals of violets, red tulips, ⟨   ⟩s, purple pansies, blue irises.

1. Soak 2 or 3 different kinds of petals in separate cups of h⟨   ⟩ for an hour. Then test each solution with vinegar for an acid and ⟨   ⟩f baking soda for a base.
2. Try some fruit juices too, like apple, plum, and var⟨   ⟩rries. You will discover that fruit juices, like flower petals, are ac⟨ ⟩

Indicator Sticks

Soak one end of a cotton swab in the red cabbage solution, the other in the green solution. Dry the swab and see if it works as an indicator for acids and bases.

The Columbus Egg

Can you make an egg balance perfectly on a level surface? Your friends will be mystified by this magic trick.

1. Hold a raw egg carefully in your hand and shake it thoroughly.

2. Now keep the egg upright between your fingers for a few minutes. You are allowing the yolk to settle on the bottom.

3. Next place the egg on a table or other level surface. It will remain upright! Can anyone guess why?

Read *Secrets of 123 Classic Science Tricks and Experiments* by E. Laners .to learn how to do other mysterious magic tricks.

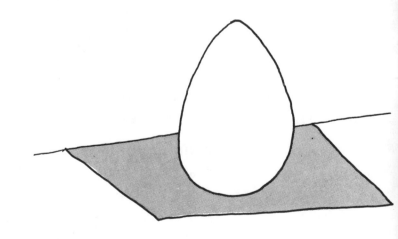

Sugar Magic

Here's a vanishing act that you'll want to practice on your friends.

1. Stir a spoonful of sugar into an inch of water in a glass and watch it dissolve. The sugar molecules are spreading through the water and seem to disappear as if by magic. Let the water dry up and the sugar will reappear.

2. With an eye dropper, put 10 drops of sugar water on a clean aluminum pie plate. Place plastic wrap or a plate on top of the pie plate. After a few minutes remove the cover and peek underneath and you will see 10 white dots!

Be sure to work over a sink, or a table covered with newspapers, for the next trick.

1. Fill a glass up to the rim with cold water.

2. Slowly pour 1 teaspoon of sugar, gently stirring with a broom straw or a thin stirrer.

3. Then add another spoonful of sugar. Has any water spilled out yet? Try another spoonful. How many can you stir in before the water overflows the glass? (If you are doing this experiment as part of a magic show, ask your audience these questions).

4. Now repeat the experiment using warm water. Which holds more sugar, warm or cold water?

5. Boiling water will hold almost 2 cups of sugar! Ask an adult to help with this experiment.

Sugar Crystals

Ask an adult to help you with the boiling water in this experiment.

YOU NEED:

1 cup boiling water

2 cups sugar

3 jars, 3 pencils, 3 paper clips, 3 6" pieces of string

Food coloring

YOU DO:

1. Make a sugar solution by adding the sugar to the boiling water. Let it boil until the sugar is dissolved. Turn off heat.

2. Let the sugar solution cool and pour it into the 3 jars.

3. Fasten the paper clips to the pieces of string; then tie the other ends around the pencils.

4. Place a pencil across each jar, letting the string and clip dangle into the water. Wait a few hours and see what happens. (Sugar crystals will form on the string.) If you are doing this trick as part of your show, you will have to prepare the jars ahead of time, so you will have a finished product to show.

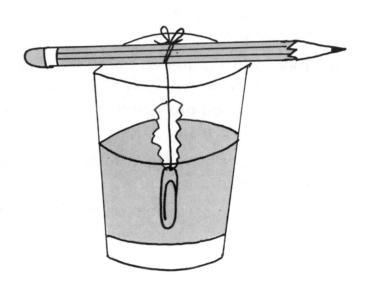

5. Put the jars in a safe place for about a month. (Don't forget they are there.) When the time is up, lift out each string and you will have a sparkling necklace of crystal gems!

6. Tie 2 long strings to each end for a necklace—2 short strings, for sparkling earrings.

ADD-ONS:

Try putting food coloring in the sugar water to make colorful crystals. These are wonderful for dress-up, to give as a gift, or to put in a jar for a dazzling display.

For quick crystals: Put 2 tablespoons of salt into 5 tablespoons of cold water. Let stand until the liquid clears. Pour into a saucer and soon crystals will appear.

Wait a few days, then lift out the largest crystals. Put them in a new solution of salt and water. Watch them grow. Keep doing this until you have grown a giant crystal.

Experiment with other household chemicals such as washing soda, Epsom salts, borax, boric acid. Dissolve each in boiling water . . . watch and see what shapes each solution makes.

After you have made 5 or 6 crystals, clear and in colors, display them in a glass bowl or dish.

Sticky Bubbles

While you are at it, you might want to blow some soap and water bubbles.

YOU NEED:

- 1 teaspoon shampoo or dishwashing liquid
- 2 tablespoons water
- A little pancake syrup
- Bubble pipes, large wands, plastic 6-pack holders
- Straw with a slant cut on the end, paper cup or plate with a hole cut in the middle, etc.

YOU DO:

1. Mix shampoo or dishwashing liquid with water and syrup. Stir gently or you will get a froth! You don't need a lot of this mixture to make millions of bubbles.
2. Have a contest and see who can blow the biggest bubbles, make a long spray of bubbles, catch the most (wet hands won't break them

as quickly), blow the most from one giant bubble blower.

3. Experiment with other bubble solutions and holders, including your hands. Make a giant bubble by placing your fingers together with thumbs and forefingers touching. Dip down into the bubble solution, quickly flip your hands out, and blow.

WIND AND WEATHER

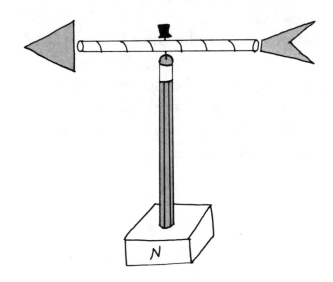

Do you listen to the weather person on television or the radio? How often has your baseball game, picnic, or outing been spoiled, because the sunny day that was predicted turned into a rainy one? Despite the use of satellites, radar detectors, and supercomputers, meteorologists (weather scientists) admit that they still can have trouble predicting what the weather will be.

It sometimes is harder to tell if a bad thunderstorm is on its way tomorrow than to predict what the general weather will be 5 days ahead. The most accurate weather prediction still comes from temperature, air pressure, humidity, and wind readings recorded with balloons launched every 12 hours from 100 places in the U.S.

Simple Weather Vane

The North Wind doth blow
And we will have snow . . .

How can you tell in what direction the wind is blowing? A weather vane will tell you, by the direction its arrow is pointing. For example, if it points toward the south, the wind is coming from the south. This sometimes means warmer weather is on its way. In the early years of our country, before sophisticated weather predictors were invented, people had beautiful handmade weather vanes perched on top of their houses. These are now sought-after collector's items.

You can make a simple weather vane:

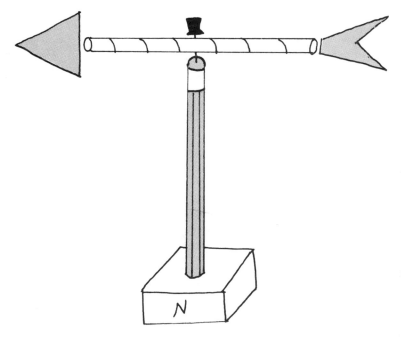

1. Push a straight pin through the middle of a drinking straw and then into the center of an eraser of an unsharpened pencil.

2. Attach a cardboard pointer and a tail.

3. Take your weathervane outside and watch it move around in the wind. What direction is it pointing? Where is the wind coming from? (Answer: the vane points in the same direction from which the wind is coming.)

4. Push the pencil into a square of styrofoam or a small box with a lid and write the four directions on it: N, E, S, W.

How can you tell which direction is which when you don't already know?

- The sun rises in the East and sets in the West. The big dipper and the North Star are in the North.

- Moss grows on the north side of a rock or tree. Trees tend to lean towards the North.

- Look at an atlas and see where your town is . . . do you have a lake or an ocean or some mountains to let you know the direction?

- Do you live on a street that goes East and West, or North and South?

Wind Anemometer

Have you ever heard the expression, "Speedy as the wind?" Weather forecasters use an anemometer to measure how hard the wind is blowing. You can make one too.

YOU NEED:

2 long strips of heavy cardboard (about 2" x 12" long)

4 sturdy paper cups, 3 of 1 color, 1 of another

Ball point pen top with clasp removed

Pencil or wooden dowel

Headless finishing nail, 2" or longer

Ruler, marker

Sharp scissors or X-Acto knife

Tape or glue

Timer or stopwatch

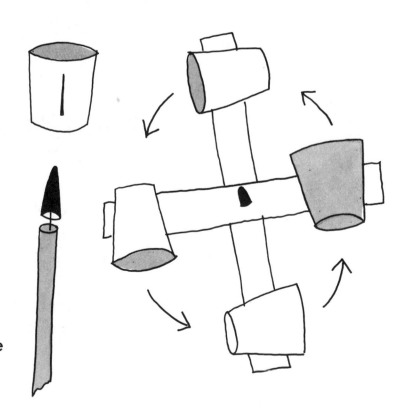

YOU DO:

1. Measure and cut out the cardboard strips. Then tape or glue them securely together at the middle.

2. With the point of a scissors or an X-Acto knife, cut a ½" inch hole through the middle. Push the pen top through. (It should fit snugly.)

3. Measure ¼ of the way up the cups from the bottom edge and make a slit on 2 opposite sides of each cup, the same size as the width of the strips. (See illustration.)

4. Slip a cup onto each end of the cardboard cross, being sure each faces in the same direction. About ½" of the cardboard should stick out.

5. Push the nail into the eraser part of the pencil and hang the cross and cups on it. Then take your anemometer outside into the wind.

6. Holding the wind instrument at arm's length, watch it spin around! Use a timer or a stopwatch and count how many times the *odd* colored cup comes around in front of you during a 2½ minute period. This will tell you the approximate speed of the wind in miles per hour. For example, if the cups go around 10 times, the wind speed is 10 mph.

ADD-ONS:

To make a sturdier anemometer, you could use a lightweight wood or lattice instead of cardboard (and a hand drill for the hole), and a longer wooden dowel for the base. Then you could stick the anemometer into the ground instead of holding it.

Rain Gauge

April showers bring May flowers
It's raining, it's pouring, the old man is snoring
Rain, rain, go away; come again another day

Everyone knows these familiar refrains. But how do we know how much rain has fallen after a big storm? You can make a simple rain gauge to measure the water.

YOU NEED:

2 jars with straight sides, a tall, narrow one and a shorter, fat one

Measuring cup, funnel

Ruler, marker

Water

YOU DO:

1. Pour 1" or centimeter of water into the short jar.

2. Transfer this water into the tall jar and mark off the amount into 10 equal parts. Each one will be ¹⁄₁₀ of an inch or centimeter. You have now calibrated the tall jar.

3. Place the funnel in the mouth of the tall jar and you will have a simple rain gauge. Take the fat jar outside and leave it there until the next rainstorm.

4. After the rain has ended, pour the water from the fat jar through the funnel into the thin jar. Then look and see how much water is in the thin jar.

5. Read off the measure. If it is at the ⁴⁄₁₀ mark, that means ⁴⁄₁₀ of an inch of rain fell during the storm.

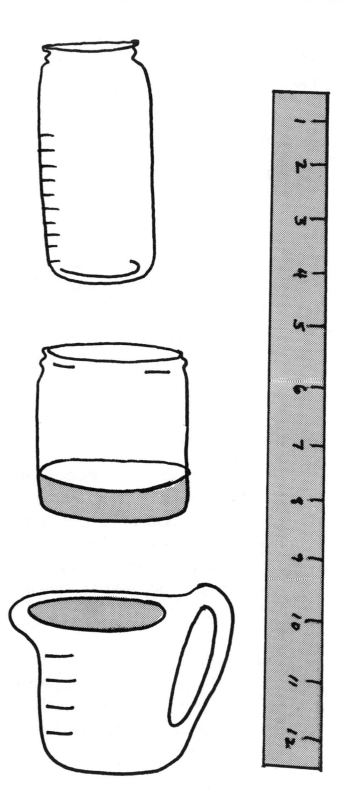

Make a Water Windmill

Did you ever see a tall metal tower with a windmill on top that turns in the breeze? Maybe you thought it is used for cooling off cattle, as some children do. Windmills are mainly used for pumping water. Because of windmills, the pioneers were able to settle wherever they wanted to in the West, instead of having to be near a lake or a stream.

You can make a windmill to play with or use as part of a farm diorama or a 3-D scene.

YOU NEED:

Small cardboard box or
    shoebox lid

5 cardboard coat hanger
    tubes, about 16" long

1 6" nail or sinker

Modeling clay

Cardboard, file cards

Toothpicks, scissors, tape

YOU DO:

1. Use a small box or a shoebox lid turned upside down for the base. Poke 4 cardboard hanger tubes through it to form the body of your windmill. Pull the tubes together at the top, teepee style but not too tight, and secure with tape.

2. Cut a stiff piece of cardboard about 5" square to be the windmill platform. Cut a hole right in the middle of the square, a little bigger than the diameter of the taped tubes. Push the cardboard down over the tubes until it fits tight.

3. Cut the 5th cardboard tube in half. Push it down through the hole in the cardboard platform so that the teepee and the cardboard hold it tight. It should stick up about 5" above the platform. If the tube is wobbly, the hole in

your platform is too big. You can reinforce your tower with tape or with toothpicks poked through the cardboard tubes to hold them tight.

4. Poke a 6" nail carefully through the tube that sticks up above the platform, about 1" from the top of the tube. This nail will hold the windmill wheel.

5. Draw and cut out long triangle shapes from file cards or light cardboard to make fan blades. Glue the triangles onto toothpicks. You will probably need 10 or 12 blades.

6. Press some modeling clay around the head of the nail and stick the toothpicks into it in a circular pattern to form the windmill wheel. Press a little more clay around the pointed end of the nail and stick 2 more slightly longer blades into that to form the tail vane. You may need to slide the nail a bit further through the cardboard tube to balance it. Or you can balance it by adding a little more clay at the light end.

7. Take your windmill outside and see if it will turn in the wind. In a real water windmill, the motion of the wheel makes a long shaft in the center of the tower go up and down to pump water from a well or water tank.

ADD-ONS:

Make an old-fashioned windmill house, the kind you see in Holland and the eastern part of the United States. Fashion the house from a shoebox that you stand on end. Save the box lid to form the back wall of the house, but don't put it on yet. Cut a door and windows in the box, not too high up. You need a big space at the top for the windmill blades or sails.

Cut out 4 large rectangular blades from file cards or light cardboard. Push a brad fastener through all 4 blades and then through the front wall of the house. Close the fastener and then put the shoebox lid on, taping securely. Put bushes, a bench, and some tiny people outside your windmill house.

Weather Myths

People used to make up stories and myths to explain the weather. Some of these seem actually to be better at predicting the weather than complicated instruments and machines.

Here are some examples:

- Aching bones or joints mean that rain is on the way.

- A halo around the moon means rain.

- "Red sky at night, sailor's delight; red sky in the morning, sailor's warning." (Change the red to pink and it is almost true, as the dust and moisture in fair-weather clouds filter out the blue, leaving a pinkish color.)

- Half a herd of cows lying down means a 50 percent chance of rain—probably it just means tired cows!

Does your family or class at school know of any other weather tales or folklore? It would be fun to make a list of them, or illustrate them and put them in a book, and wait to see if any come true.

Experiments in Aerodynamics

Aerodynamics is the study of the way objects behave in the air. Birds, kites, and airplanes are all subject to the laws of aerodynamics.

Here are some simple experiments to try.

YOU NEED:

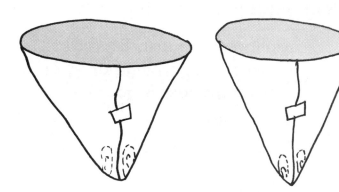

- 2 paper circles about 8″ in diameter, or 2 cone-shaped coffee filters
- Paper clips
- Clear tape

YOU DO:

1. Cut, fold, and tape 2 circles of paper into cone shapes. Use the same amount of tape on each one.

2. Put 2 paper clips into each cone and then, holding one in each hand, let both of them drop to the floor or ground. Watch to see what happens.

3. Next, take the clips out of 1 of the cones. Drop them again. Which one hits the ground first?

4. Turn one cone upside down and clip 2 paper clips on opposite edges. Now drop the 2 cones. What happens? The cone with its nose down is faster. The other one acts as a parachute.

5. Try adding more paper clips to the parachute cone. How many did you add before it caught up with the nose cone?

6. What else could you do to speed up the flight, or slow it down?

Parachutes

Make several parachutes by attaching different-sized spools or wooden clothespins to the 4 corners of a handkerchief with 4 pieces of string or yarn.

See which one lands first. Then make a chart of your findings. You could decorate the spools or clothespins to look like parachute people.

Paper Airplane Race

Make several paper airplanes and gliders to see which design will travel through space the fastest.

YOU NEED:

Lightweight paper, 8½" x 11" (onionskin, typing paper, or tracing paper is good)

Paper clips

Crayons or markers

YOU DO:

Bird Glider

1. To make a bird glider, fold a piece of paper lengthwise. Unfold the paper, turn it over, and fold the top corners into the center, as shown in the illustration.

2. Next, fold each side in towards the center to about ½" from the mid-line. Open, turn over, and bend each side or wing down at the outer line. Can you see an airplane or bird shape?

3. Hold the bird glider underneath the wings, along the creased edge, with your thumb and forefinger, and let it fly. Does it go straight? Try putting a paper clip on the nose or beak. What happens now?

Rabbit Glider

1. Make another glider. This time add rabbit ears to the wings. Fold a 5" x 5" square of paper on the diagonal. Open it and cut along the crease. Fold the triangle in half.

2. Draw a line ⅜" along the top from the top edge. Fold each "ear" up at the line. Cut off the tip and slip a paper clip on the bottom edge.

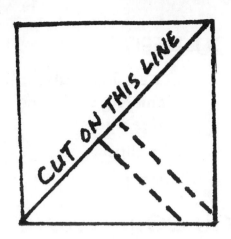

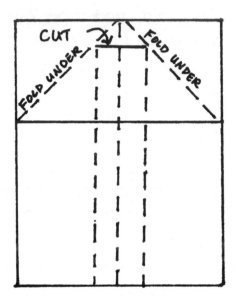

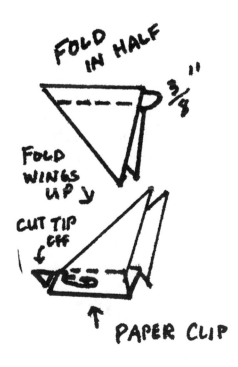

94

3. Insert the ears in the body of the glider, and secure with tape. Now launch your Rabbit Glider into the air. Does it fly straight? Will it beat the bird glider in a race through space? Why do you think ears and more weight will help a glider or airplane fly faster and straighter?

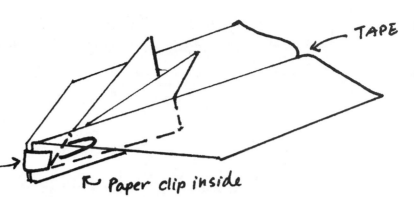

Tape →

TAPE

Paper clip inside

ADD-ONS:

Make some other airplanes, including ones of balsa wood, with sleek wings and tail and a pointed nose. Have fun flying your planes with your friends. If you are really ambitious, put together some model airplane kits to display in your room or give as a gift.

KITES

Children and grownups have been fascinated by kite-flying from the earliest days. There are hundreds of different kinds of kites that can be made, from a simple paper and string version, to the complicated 4-line stunt kites popular today. These come equipped with 2 handles and double strings, and are being flown any place with lots of open space—large school playgrounds, empty parking lots, beaches, and open fields.

Here are several kinds of kites for you to try constructing.

Bow-and-Arrow Bird Kite

Kite-making is a very satisfying wintertime activity. Here is one that you can design and put together while waiting for the spring winds to blow.

YOU NEED:

> 5 bamboo stakes or slats, each about 24" long
>
> Medium-weight string
>
> Lightweight paper
>
> Scraps of colored tissue paper, construction paper, or cloth
>
> X-Acto knife or scissors, markers, stapler, glue

YOU DO:

1. Cut a notch in each end of a piece of bamboo (from an old window shade or your garden center) and stretch a string between the notches. The result will be a bow shape.

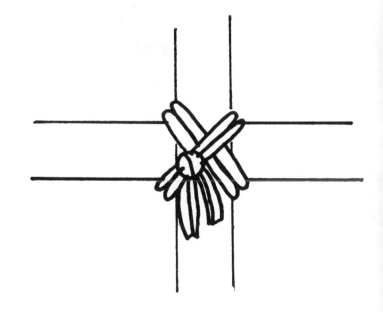

2. Glue and tie or lash together 3 long and 1 short bamboo slat into a teepee shape, as shown in the illustration. Then secure it to the bow the same way. Can you see a birdlike shape?

3. Cut light-weight paper (plastic wrap, tissue, rice, typing paper) into a shape a little larger than the frame, and decorate it, if you wish, with colored markers, tissue collage, or construction paper. Then glue the shape onto the bamboo frame. Add a cloth or crepe paper tail.

4. Tie on a string bridle, and hang your bird kite on your wall until it's time to get it out and go flying.

Grocery Bag Kite

Here's an easy kite to make from a grocery or lunch bag. All you need are a ball of cotton string, some tape, a ruler, and a pencil or markers.

YOU DO:

1. First, cut off the bottom of the bag and throw it away. Measure the length of the bottomless bag along the seam where it is glued. Make a mark ⅓ down from the top.

2. Put an X of tape over the mark; then measure ¼" from each corner of the bag and put a dot there. Make lines from the 4 dots to the X of tape, as shown in the illustration. Cut along the lines on this side only. Don't cut through both sides of the bag.

3. Spread these "wings" out, then turn the bag over and tape the wings to the body. Punch a hole in the tip of each wing and tape just

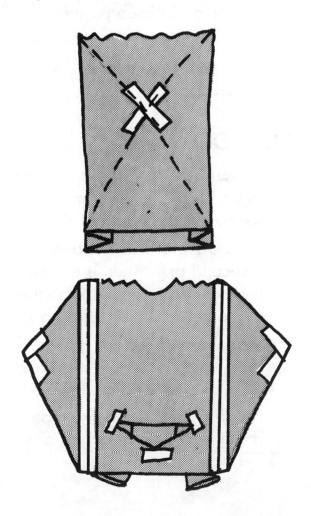

above it, as shown.

4. Draw and cut out a triangle near the bottom of the body, and reinforce the corners with tape.

5. Tie a string 6 feet long through each hole; then tie on your flying line or ball of string to the center of the bridle. You might want to roll the string onto a stick or wooden handle.

6. Now your kite is all set to fly! Decorate it, if you wish.

Drinking Straw Kite

YOU NEED:

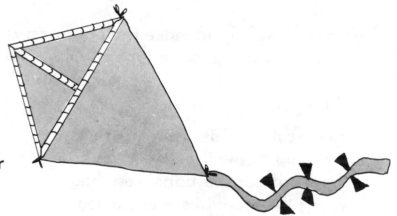

6 sturdy drinking straws

Typing or tissue paper

Crepe paper

A ball of lightweight string

Scissors, glue, tape, stapler

YOU DO:

1. Attach 3 of the straws together into a triangle shape by threading a long string through them and securely tying a knot at each end. (Hint: if you gently suck one end of the straw, the string will come through.)

2. Thread 2 more straws and add them to one side of the first triangle to form a second one. Then use tape or string to connect the remaining straw from the top of the second triangle to the bottom of the first triangle. This makes a geometric shape called a *tetrahedron*.

3. Measure and cut out typing or tissue paper to cover 2 sides of the kite and tape, glue, or staple it around the straws. (You might want to draw or glue on a decoration first.)

4. Tie on a long tissue or crepe paper tail to the bottom of the kite. Attach a string bridle and the ball of string, and your drinking straw kite is ready to fly!

Basic Diamond-Shaped Kite

Kites are a little like birds. In fact, the name kite comes from a bird of the same name in the hawk family. A flying paper kite looks a little like a graceful kite bird gliding through the air. Although kites come in every shape, the most traditional one is shaped like a diamond. Enjoy making this one, or experiment with other shapes such as a hexagon, box, fish, or animal. The sky's the limit!

YOU NEED:

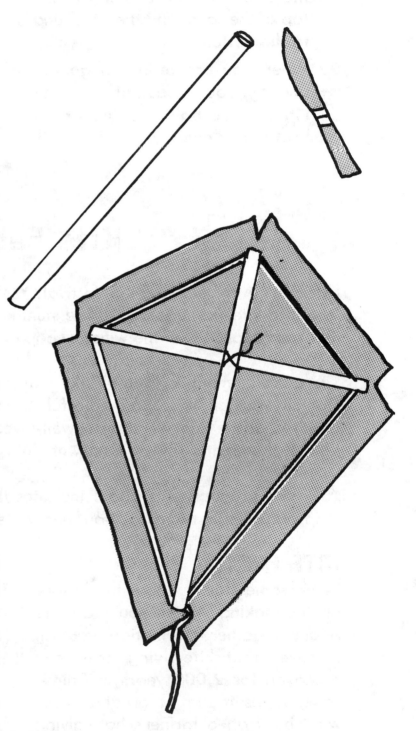

2 lightweight sticks, dowels or pine lattice

Typing paper, newsprint, wrapping or tissue paper

Cloth scraps or crepe paper strips

Nylon cord or heavy string

Markers, acrylic paint diluted with water

Scissors, penknife, stapler, glue

Ball of kite string

YOU DO:

1. To make the kite frame, cut small slits in the ends of the sticks.

2. Securely lash together the 2 sticks, as in illustration. Then stretch a long string taut through the slits to form the frame.

3. Lay the frame down on paper and draw around it, leaving an extra inch or so all around. If you cut V-shapes out of each corner, the paper will go around the sticks better.

4. Before attaching the paper cover to the frame, decorate it, if you wish. Then carefully fold down

edges and glue or staple them to the sticks. Reinforcing the edges with tape is a good idea.

5. Tie a few cloth or crepe paper strips together for a tail and attach it to the kite.

6. Finally, cut a length of string for the bridle and tie one end to the top of the spine and the other end to the bottom.

7. When you are ready to go out and fly your beautiful diamond kite, tie the ball of string to the bridle, and away you go!

Kite Festival

Have you ever been to a kite festival? You will see everything there from tiny 6-inch bird kites to huge decorative stunt kites that float through the air, sparkle like stars, dance with the wind, swoop and dive like butterflies and swallows.

There are so many kites in the sky that it almost looks painted! At a festival in Hawaii you might see 52 colorful "Hyperkites" stacked up on top of one another, as the hats were in the well-loved book, *Caps For Sale*; or ribbons of light in the night sky from kites with lights attached.

Ask your grandparents about the kites they made, as children, out of comic strip pages, split bamboo, flour-and-water paste, and scraps of string.

KITE FACTS:

Write some stories about the history of kite-making. When you read kite books to gather information, you will discover that kite-flying has been going on for 2,000 years in China. Legend has it that a great gust of wind blew off a farmer's hat, giving him the idea to attach a cord to another hat and launch it in the air.

The Japanese phrase *tako kichi* means kite-crazy.

Write some kite poems like this one:

I love to fly my kite so high,
above the tree tops in the sky.
Circling and looping ever so free,
I really wish it could be me.

In modern-day China, the kite festival at Weifang attracts thousands of visitors from around the world, eager to see the main attraction, a huge 150-foot dragon made of hand-painted silk, with "bones" of bamboo.

Benjamin Franklin's famous kite was nothing more than a large handkerchief stretched between two cedar sticks.

Before Marco Polo left on a voyage, a man would be tied to a kite and launched from the deck of the ship. If he was carried aloft, it was a good omen and the voyage could depart.

There is also a story of two young boys who flew over the palace of an Assyrian king in an "eagle" or kite, bearing stones and mortar to build a castle in the air.

OTHER FACTS ABOUT KITES:

Guatemalan Indians make 30-foot round kites with bright-colored paper stretched on a 12-spoke frame. They fly them over cemeteries in honor of the dead on All Souls Day, November 2.

Japanese Kites

A favorite kite of Japanese children is a large paper crane, similar to the small ones they string into necklaces.

They also fly a rectangular kite called *Play Sail,* which looks like a huge, many-colored patchwork quilt. It is held at the four corners until the wind catches it, and puffs it up like an inflated balloon.

GARDENING AND NATURE

Vegetable and Flower Garden

There is nothing quite as satisfying as planning, planting, and tending one's own garden. Begin early in the season, and by late summer and early fall, you will have beautiful flowers to enjoy, and vegetables to share with your family and friends.

YOU NEED:

A small plot of land

Garden tools

Seeds, fertilizer

Watering can or hose

Sticks, string, marking pen

YOU DO:

1. It's fun to look through garden books and catalogs to plan your outdoor garden. After you have decided on what you want, draw a diagram showing where everything will go. Keep in mind the height and spread of the various flowers and vegetables, so you can place the smaller ones in front and leave room for growing.

2. Beans and sugar snap peas will need a fence or trellis, and should be planted at the north end of your garden, if possible, so they won't block the sun. Squash, pumpkins, and watermelons need a large area.

3. You might want to use the chart below to help with your planning. In addition to *annuals* (things that must be replanted each year), you could plant some *perennials* that come up every year. Examples of these are hollyhocks, bachelor buttons, peonies, chives, and mint.

4. When the weather is right to actually plant your garden, ask your parents, or someone older than you, to help you prepare the plot. First, dig up the earth with a spade or a shovel, then turn the soil and rake well to remove debris and break up the lumps. Mix in some fertilizer or homemade compost, peat moss, and sand (to make the soil drain better).

5. When all is in readiness, mark off the rows with sticks and some string, and plant your seeds or small plants according to the directions on the seed packets or pots.

6. It's helpful to place a marker at the end of each row (staple or tape the empty packets onto popsicle or other sticks), to remind you what is growing where.

7. Water your garden well, continuing to do so whenever the soil is dry. Pull up the pesky weeds and thin out the plants if the space becomes too crowded. Before too long, your garden will come alive!

ADD-ONS:

Scatter some flower seeds, such as nasturtiums, zinnias, marigolds, and straw flowers, on a circle or square of soil, cover lightly with more soil, and water well, for a lovely scatter garden.

To discourage bugs and other garden pests, attract the birds by setting out a birdbath nearby. You can make one from a shallow dish or an upside-down garbage can cover set on a stump or block of wood. Be sure to change the water each day.

To keep the rabbits from nibbling your lettuce and cabbage leaves, sprinkle a few mothballs or plant some basil nearby. Marigolds, with their pungent smell and bright orange color, help keep away tiny worms and insects.

Rig up a scarecrow out of some sticks and your old clothes, and perch him in your garden.

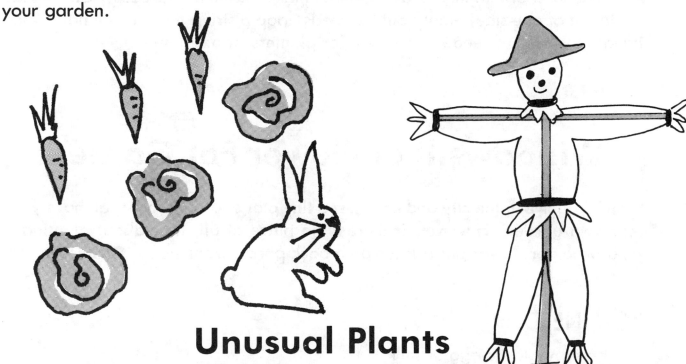

Unusual Plants

1. If you are really adventuresome, you might want to plant some unusual vegetables: blue potatoes, giant elephant garlic, yellow peppers that look like bananas, or popcorn in rainbow colors!
2. Look for the seeds at your garden center, or in a catalogue.

Thanks to *Backyard Vacation* by Haas, Cole and Natzger for some of these ideas

Hanging Gourds

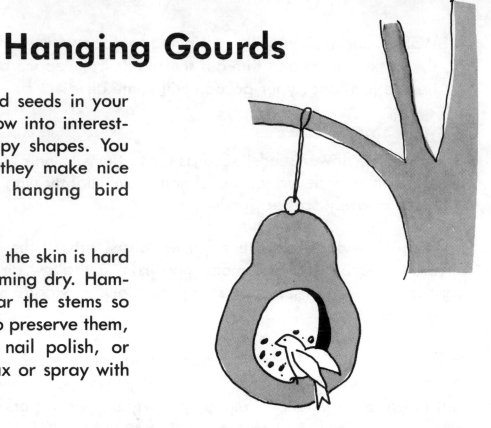

It's fun to plant gourd seeds in your garden. They will grow into interesting smooth and bumpy shapes. You can't eat them, but they make nice fall decorations or hanging bird feeders.

Pick the gourds when the skin is hard and the stem is becoming dry. Hammer 2 nail holes near the stems so they will dry faster. To preserve them, cover with colorless nail polish, or rub in some floor wax or spray with shellac.

Leave them in a cool, dry place for several weeks. Then shake them and listen for the sound of rattling seeds. (Gourds make excellent maracas.) Cut a wide circle out of one side, empty out the seeds, loop a string through the holes, and hang up your bird feeder. Use them for planters, too.

Windowsill or Flower Pot Garden

Even if you live in the city and have just a tiny plot of ground, you can have your very own garden. However, if there is no place at all, how about planting a windowbox or flower pot garden on a back porch, front stoop, terrace, or fire escape?

YOU NEED:

Empty plastic egg or milk
   cartons, paper or plastic
   cups, plastic soft drink
   containers, a tray or small
   saucers, scrap lumber

Large clay pots, plastic buckets, gallon cans

Potting soil, fertilizer, small rocks or pebbles

Nails, hammer, trowel or scoop

Vegetable and flower seeds

Sticks, paper, pen

YOU DO:

1. For a small windowsill garden, use an egg or milk carton, small paper or plastic cups, or a 2-liter plastic soft drink container, cut down to 6" or 7" high.

2. Punch holes in the bottom of the containers for drainage and line with small stones. Then spoon in soil, sprinkle a few seeds on top, cover with more soil, and water well.

3. Next stick in some wooden markers to identify the seeds and place on a tray or saucer in a sunny window. Watch for your seeds to sprout. (Germination will take place faster if you put the container in a sealed plastic bag and keep it in a warm spot out of direct sunlight for a few days.)

4. To make a sturdier window box for outdoors, nail together some boards into a planter, drill holes in the bottom for drainage, and fill with a layer of small rocks. Then follow the directions above.

5. Clay pots, buckets, and other containers also make excellent outdoor planters. Try growing geraniums, sunflowers, and even corn and tomatoes from small plants or seeds.

6. Fertilizer and a layer of peat moss on top will make your plants grow even better. As your plants become larger, thin them out a bit, pinch off some of the small flowers and leaves, and pull any weeds that appear.

7. Continue to weed and water your indoor/outdoor gardens. Soon you will have a welcome patch of green (as well as bright colors) all summer long! And what fun to harvest and eat what you have grown.

Bottle Scoop

YOU NEED:

A plastic bleach bottle with
handle, carefully washed
and rinsed

Pencil, bread knife

YOU DO:

1. Mark where the bottle needs to be cut; then carefully cut out the shape with
   the bread knife.

2. Use your scoop to shovel out sand or earth from the garden. You will find
   your new scoop to be lightweight, and it won't rust as a metal one would.

Plant Water Bottle

YOU NEED:

A large plastic soda pop bottle,
carefully washed and rinsed

Water

YOU DO:

1. Fill the bottle with water and push it upside down into the soil next to the
   plant, being sure it stands securely on its own.

2. The water will seep out slowly, keeping the plant's roots damp for several
   days. This is a good idea for vacationers or for dry spells in the summer.

Pretty Potato Face

YOU NEED:

1 large potato

Cotton balls

Bird seed

Knife

Spoon

Buttons, ribbon, tacks, pins

YOU DO:

1. Cut a slice off of the top and the bottom of a large potato. Place it on a saucer or some cardboard.

2. Next, scoop out the top of the potato and stuff damp cotton balls into the opening.

3. Sprinkle the bird seed on the cotton, and water it often so it stays moist.

4. In a few days, the bird seed will grow into curly hair.

5. Now you can add features to the potato face by pinning on buttons, tacks, colorful yarn or ribbons, or whatever you think up.

ADD-ONS:

Try the same with other vegetables such as eggplant, cucumbers, green peppers, or pumpkins and see how many characters you can create with different shapes and faces.

Autumn Nature Walk

Crisp October days are the perfect time to get outside and enjoy the brightly colored leaves of autumn. Here are some ideas to get you started.

YOU NEED:

Keen eyes, comfortable shoes, a sack lunch

Binoculars, magnifying glass, collecting bag

Notebook and pencil

Camera (optional)

111

YOU DO:

1. Make plans for a walk in the woods, along a trail, or at a nearby nature center or forest preserve. All of autumn's bright colors will be there to greet you.

2. As you stroll along, look at all of the beautiful trees and bushes. Do you know their names? You can usually identify a tree by the shape of the leaves, type of bark, and its seeds or flowers (acorns, pine cones, seed packs, petals, etc.).

3. Chances are you will see one or more of these trees: red maple, red oak, katsura, white ash (red or yellow leaves), gingko tree (vivid yellows).

4. Bushes worth spotting: juneberry and hawthorn plants (orange-red fruit), chokeberry shrub (various colored berries), staghorn sumac, which grows along roadways (yellow, orange, and red leaves with "arrowhead" shaped fruits sitting on top to attract birds).

5. Can you discover wild blueberries, flower-producing grasses, and other tall weeds? You may see yellow "false sunflowers" growing abundantly in many areas at this time of year. What other bright flowers can you spot?

6. Make sketches or snap some photos. Gather leaves, acorns, weeds, and other finds or treasures, to take home with you.

7. After you've enjoyed a picnic lunch and a rest, you'll be ready to return home to consult some nature books about all of your discoveries.

8. You'll probably want to press or dry your leaves, weeds, and flowers and make a nature book, book mark, placemats, paperweight, and other nature crafts and gifts.

Seeing the Forest Through the Trees

A forest can contain many things besides trees, although we usually only notice the trees. There are many different types of forests, including open areas, young forests, mature forests, and old growth forests such as the ancient rain forests of the Pacific Northwest.

YOU DO:

1. Take a walk with an adult through a nearby woods or forest preserve. As you go along, try to recognize the different kinds of grasses, plants, and trees. You will begin to see the forests through the trees!

2. You may start off in a grassy meadow, which is a natural open space. If you come to a place that is light and airy but has burnt tree stumps and brownish vegetation, it will probably be an open space created by lightning or a forest fire.

3. In time, these openings will return to being a forest again. A meadow with low-growing plants, weeds, and wildflowers will always be a meadow.

4. After a fire or a tree harvest (in lumbering areas), the forest may be full of small shrubs and young trees. With more sunlight, many plants can grow. If you are very lucky, you may hear birds and animals, or spot some feeding on the berries or tender leaves . . . or hiding in the thickets.

5. Young forests grow up naturally or are replanted after a fire. They make good habitats for birds and animals from turtles to deer and even bears.

6. Mature forests are crowned with leafy branches, or canopies, that keep the forest dark and cool. Only animals that can climb or fly up to the high branches, such as squirrels and owls, tend to live there. If you walk through a mature forest, it will be *very* quiet.

7. Old-growth forests are the darkest of all, because of the large trees, dead and fallen branches, and carpets of twigs, moldy leaves, pine needles, and other debris. Since it's hard for the wind to whistle through the trees, old forests protect both large and small animals. Listen and you might hear a woodpecker making pecking sounds on an old, dead tree. If you see a northern flying squirrel, you might also see a spotted owl, swooping down on it. However, there are very few spotted owls left in the Pacific Northwest, because loggers are cutting down the enormous old fir trees where they live.

8. When you return home from your walk, make a list of all of the different things you saw. Sketch some pictures of the various trees, starting with young saplings and going up to very tall and wide ones, such as the California redwoods. Look in a tree book to find some of the trees you saw on your walk.

ADD-ONS:

You might want to learn more about the animals and trees of the forests. Look at the page on endangered species to find out about the animals, birds, and plants on the list.

Do some paintings or color in drawings of different kinds of forests. What colors will you use? How many shades of green? Pay special attention to the lights and darks, shadows and highlights.

Camouflaged Nature Hunt

This game is best played outdoors, but can also be adapted as an indoor hunt.

YOU NEED:

> Paper, pencil
> Objects from nature
> Unnatural objects

YOU DO:

1. Gather together 5 or 6 unnatural objects to be hidden along a trail, or in your backyard or playground. These might include: a balloon, paper-weight, paper leaves or flowers, a yo yo, alarm clock, etc.

2. Before the hunt begins, hide the objects along the trail in places where they can easily be seen (for younger children), or in harder places (for older ones).

3. Divide into teams and give each a pencil and pad of paper. Set a time limit for the hunt.

4. At a signal, each team starts out along the trail to find the unnatural objects hidden there. When a team member spots a planted object, he or she points to it and waits until the captain comes and writes down the name. Don't touch the object and be as quiet as possible about the discovery.

5. The team that discovers all of the hidden objects first is the winner. Award prizes, if you wish.

Here is a way to make the hunt harder. Hide objects of the same colorings as the hiding place (e.g. green, brown, yellow); put paper leaves or flowers in among real ones, pretend moss on top of real moss, a brown lollipop on top of a brown rock, etc. See how well you can camouflage the items.

To play these games again and again, take turns hiding the various objects for the others to discover.

Visit a Botanical Garden

If you are lucky enough to live near a botanical garden, you will find it a magical place, with beautiful trees, bushes, flowers, and even waterfalls. There are no language barriers in such a place, because everyone enjoys getting close to nature, digging in the earth, and helping things grow and flourish.

When you visit there, you will see plants native to your city, as well as rare and exotic ones from far-off places. Whether it be tomatoes, desert cactus plants, rare orchids, or Amazon lilies, gardening encourages people to work together and to enjoy nature.

1. On your visit, be sure to bring along a notebook and pencil, a camera or sketchbook, and perhaps a sack lunch to eat on a bench or a grassy bank.

2. Come equipped with questions to ask about *your* neighborhood (e.g. What are hardy city trees? How can you plant a window box garden, a Japanese dish garden, or a bonsai tree? What about nurturing back stoop tomatoes or planting a small vegetable garden?)

3. While you are touring the garden, be sure to sketch or take some pictures of interesting kinds of flora and fauna, jot down notes, and try to discover the answers to your questions.

4. When you get home, you can turn all of your new-found knowledge into nature games, a scrapbook, some botanical stationery or note cards, an illustrated book, or a picture to decorate your room.

BIRDS AND ANIMALS

Play host to visiting birds by helping them with nest building, constructing a birdhouse and feeder, and providing food and water.

Birdhouse

1. General rules: Except for purple martins, who like being with other martins, most birds prefer single-family houses, placed far apart.

2. Construct your house of wood (metal is much too hot), set the opening or door away from the wind and high off the floor of the house to protect the baby birds. Drill holes at the top for ventilation. The roof should slope and have an overhang so the rain can run off. Paint or stain your house in light earth tones, even though you may like bright colors better.

A Bluebird House

You will really help out the bluebirds if you build a special house for them. Just follow the illustrations below and be sure to make the entrance hole no bigger than 1 ½" wide, so other birds can't get in.

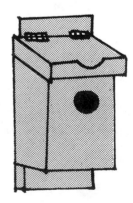

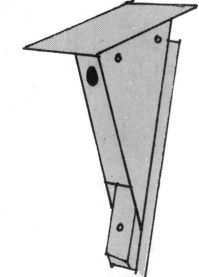

By hinging the roof, you can open it up and clean the house out. Ventilation holes under the roof will keep the air circulating, and drainage holes on the bottom will keep it dry.

If you paint black holes on the top and sides of the house, the flying bluebirds will be attracted more quickly to your birdhouse.

Hang your birdhouse up as high as you can (a steel post in the backyard is best), and wait for the bluebirds to find it!

Robin's Roost

Robins and barn swallows prefer an open shelter like the one in the illustration (about 11″ × 11″ × 8 ½″). This large, open house will help you to see what's going on, too.

Make yours out of scrap wood or ¾″ rough-cut pine. Walnut stain will make it last longer.

Hang it on a tree, on the side of a building, or under an overhanging roof. How soon will the first birds of spring arrive at your roost?

Nests

1. Most birds have both a summer and a winter home, often returning to the same places every spring. And each new generation of bird parents construct their nests the same way as their parents did. For example, robins use mud and hummingbirds like spider webs to hold their nests together. Females are the builders in the bird kingdom.

2. Give the birds some help with nest-building early in the spring by setting aside a small area of your yard for bits of cloth, straw, string, yarn, and cotton (but not a spider web, unless you're lucky enough to find one)!

3. The best time to collect nests is in the late fall after the bird families have left and the trees are bare. Don't feel you are stealing the nest, because birds never use the same one twice. Spray on a coat of shellac to preserve your nest, mount it on a forked branch, and display it in your nature collection.

Feeding the Birds

1. Look around your kitchen and you're sure to find lots of odds 'n ends to keep your bird feeder full: crumbs of bread, crackers, and cake; bits of leftover cereal and popcorn, even a stale doughnut to hang on a string.

2. Sparrows and cardinals will eat only seeds, robins prefer berries and fruit.

3. Try these bird food recipes:

   Mix raisins, bread crumbs, leftover cooked oatmeal and potatoes together in a paper or plastic cup, empty tuna tin, or cottage cheese container. Pour a little bacon grease over the mixture and let it harden. Visiting birds will love this pudding.

   Mix together 2 cups of yellow cornmeal, 2 cups of sugar, 2 cups of ground suet, with a cup of flour and 2 cups of water. Cook for 5 minutes, stirring occasionally. Keep in the refrigerator, putting a little out each day.

4. Your local health food, garden, or nature store, or even the supermarket will have packaged bird seed to use, along with your homemade delicacies.

5. During cold winters birds will depend on you to feed them. Once you start feeding them, however, and they keep coming back, be sure to continue. Leave a dish of fresh water out too, somewhere near the feeder and away from squirrels and other pests.

Milk Carton Feeder

YOU NEED:

Empty plastic milk carton or
bleach bottle

Aluminum pie plates, wire
  hanger with a cardboard
  tube

Rope, scissors, or X-Acto knife

Tape, glue, markers

YOU DO:

1. Use a large milk carton or an empty plastic bottle for the holder. Cut a large hole in the side for a door. If you leave the door attached at the top, you'll have a flap to keep out the rain.

2. Attach a pie plate to the bottom with glue or tape, and another to the top to make a roof. Or cut out a roof from another milk carton. Stick the tube from the hanger through for a perch and use the top part for hanging up your feeder.

3. Write your name, address, or a message on the front. Fill your bird feeder with seeds or other tidbits, and wait patiently until some birds discover your home-made feeder.

ADD-ONS:

Think up some other feeders to make from junk materials. Hang up a berry basket, mesh potato or onion bag, a scooped-out gourd, or a grapefruit rind, and fill them with seeds, crumbs, and/or suet. Spread peanut butter or suet on a pine cone, or even on a stale doughnut, and hang them up.

Automatic Feeder

This feeder can be used for animals or birds that eat seeds.

YOU NEED:

    2 large plastic bleach bottles,
        carefully washed
    Scissors
    2 loops of wire

YOU DO:

1. Cut the bottom off one bottle to make a bowl.

2. Cut the other bottle ¾ through the bottom to make a lid on the feeder.

3. Join the feeder to the side of a cage or fence with 2 loops of wire, 1 at the neck of the bottle and 1 in the center.

4. The bottle neck should be placed a bit above the bottom of the bowl so that the seed doesn't run out at once.

5. Watch your feeder daily and replace the seed when it runs low.

ADD-ONS:

Outdoor animals will especially appreciate the feeder in the wintertime when food is scarce. Place your feeder near a window or use binoculars to observe the animals that come to eat.

Bird Watching

1. Once you've attracted the neighborhood birds to your yard, spend some time observing their habits. The spring is an exciting time, as birds court, mate, nest, and feed their young then. Only early birds will catch a glimpse of the dawn feedings, between 4:00 and 7:00 a.m.!

2. If you're really adventurous, you'll go on an early morning bird walk to try to spot some of the 800 different kinds of bird species in North America. Dress in dull-colored clothes, not bright ones, and wear sturdy waterproof shoes. Pick a clear day, and always keep the rising sun at your back, if you can, to see the birds in their full colors.

3. Bring along binoculars, a bird book, notebook, pencil, camera, and a carry-along breakfast. Move slowly and quietly, freezing when you spot an unusual bird. You can attract its attention by making a squeaky sound against the back of your hand, or with a reed or a bird whistle.

4. When you get home, write up your notes, make a picture from your sketches, and develop your film (or take it to a camera shop). Then you can put together a bird watching book.

The World Series of Bird Watching

Did you know that, just as there is a baseball world series, there's also a world series of bird watching? It takes place in New Jersey in the springtime. Thirty, or more, teams of bird watchers gather to see which one can spot the most birds. Their contest lasts for 24 hours, beginning at midnight, but yours can be any time.

YOU NEED:

Binoculars, pad of paper, pencil

Tape recorder, camera, telescope (optional)

Drab but warm clothing

Bird book, sharp eyes and ears.

YOU DO:

1. Divide into two or more teams. Decide on a date, time, and place for this unusual competition. Early morning is best, but you can plan yours for the most convenient time.

2. Establish the ground rules:
   • Everyone on the team must either see or hear a particular bird.
   • The team that spots and/or hears the most bird species wins.
   • Prizes are awarded (a bird book, bird picture or sculpture, birdhouse, etc.), along with a treat for the entire group at the end. The New Jersey contest awards a silver cup and a statuette of binoculars embedded in stone.

3. At a signal, the teams set off into the woods, nature trail, seashore, or wherever birds are found in your community.

4. It's a good idea to dress for the weather (e.g. coat, boots, hat, sun glasses, long pants) and take along a snack and a cool drink, if the bird watching will last several hours.

5. Once a bird is spotted or heard, everyone must stand still and be very quiet so all of the team members can see, hear, and identify the species of bird. Tape recording the bird's call is a good idea, if you can. Try to get a snapshot of the bird too, just in case there is a problem later. You will also have something exciting to put in your scrapbook or bird journal.

6. Who will be the winning team? At the 1989 bird watching world series, the team that won saw or heard 200 species of birds!

7. When time is up, gather back at the starting place and compare notes, recordings, and pictures (sketches or Polaroid shots).

8. Sit down and enjoy refreshments, then award the prizes.

ADD-ONS:

Make a scrapbook and/or journal of the bird hunt. Draw and frame pictures, and write a story about the day's events. Read books about the birds. Make a birdhouse, bird feeder, or birdbath.

This would make an unusual kind of birthday party, at any time of year. There are winter birds around in most parts of the country.

Bird and Animal Guessing Games

Play these games with friends of all ages, during free time, at a birthday party, or special school or family occasion.

YOU NEED:

Index cards, pencils, crayons

Magazine pictures, glue

YOU DO:

1. Play this guessing game with just two people or a group. First, do some research on groups of birds and animals: classify them into fishes, amphibians, reptiles, birds, or mammals; find out if they are warm-blooded (birds and mammals) or cold-blooded (fishes, amphibians, reptiles); where they live, what they eat, what kinds of tracks they make; if they are predators; their distinctive characteristics, etc. Then you will know what questions to ask and movements to make.

2. Using index cards, write down the names and/or draw or glue on pictures of animals and birds. The older the group, the harder the bird or animal.

3. Pin or tape a card on the back of each player. At a signal the players take turns asking questions about what bird or animal they represent. For example, "Do I have feathers, eat seeds, and live in a tree?" "Am I cold-blooded, a predator, with large paws?" How quickly can you identify who you are?

4. After each bird or animal has been tracked down, collect the cards and have the players break into two or more teams. Then play a game of Charades, with each team guessing who the other team is by their sounds and movements.

5. Play a Noah's Ark Game by giving each person the name or picture of a bird or animal. The object is to find your partner through actions and sounds. Bedlam may occur as all of the birds and animals screech, whistle, bark, yell, and cavort around, madly stamping, flapping, jumping, and acting wild. Who will be the last to find a partner?

6. Play a Camouflage Game by taking turns hiding behind, under, or beside something that is the same shape or color you are. Set a time limit for the searchers to find the hidden animals and birds. Stay very still, but let out a few animal noises once in a while. If someone goes right past, jump out and demonstrate who you are by your movements and noises.

7. Playing this game outdoors on a moonlit night, or just at dusk, is even harder and more fun. Can you hide in the shadows? Will your clothing blend into the bushes? Bring along flashlights and try spotting the hidden birds or animals. Be sure to play this game in a safe place.

Zoo Cards

1. Before making a visit to the zoo, create some Zoo Cards that contain questions about the animals and birds you will see there. Then during your visit, try to find the answers.

2. Here are some examples:
   How many pounds does a baby gorilla weigh?
   What do sea lions eat?
   What color is a toucan?
   Where do panda bears come from?
   How about black bears?
   What do Snowy owls do during the night?

3. Draw or glue on pictures of the various animals, birds, and sea creatures to illustrate the cards. Then your younger brothers and sisters can spot them quickly.

4. When you get home, sort out all of the cards and other information you picked up at the zoo, and write in the answers. Make up some new cards, based on things you learned.

5. Write some zoo stories and poems, make a book or a scrapbook, sing some zoo songs, turn the zoo cards into a lotto or other board game.

Zoo-Ography

Create some silly zoo creatures by combining parts of your favorite birds and animals (or imaginary ones), and play some funny games.

YOU NEED:

Paper, cardboard, or file cards

Zoo pictures from magazines or other games

Pencil, crayons, or felt-tip markers

Scissors, glue

YOU DO:

1. Divide or fold a piece of paper or cardboard into 3 parts, or use file cards. Draw or glue on the head of an animal on the top section, the body in the middle one, and the legs and feet on the bottom.

2. Label them 1, 2, 3 and cut them apart.

3. Next, sort your animal parts into 3 piles and you're ready to put together some silly puzzles. Make up nonsense names for the animals you create. Keep playing this game until you've used up all of the combinations.

4. Play a wacky zoo game by shuffling all of the cards and having each player, in turn, pick one. Whenever someone collects the 3 different parts, he or she puts them down, so everyone can laugh at the wacky animals. Keep playing until all of the cards have been picked.

5. Another version of this game is to pass around a sheet of paper and let each player draw a part of a zoo animal. For example, the first person starts out by drawing a head, then passes the paper along to the next player, who folds the paper down and draws a body. The third player adds legs and feet, and so on until everyone has had a chance to add a part. Then open up the paper and see all the silly creatures your group has created!

Endangered Species

Did you know that pandas, cactus, and spotted owls are on the endangered species list? We hear a lot about animals and birds that no longer exist or are close to disappearing. These, along with 200 plants and flowers, are called "endangered species." Many naturalists are trying to save them, including the people at the San Diego and other Zoos, by raising them under ideal conditions, or in habitats and environments close to the natural ones where they live. Learn more about endangered species.

1. Call or visit your local zoo, botanical garden, or nature conservatory to discover more about these endangered birds, plants, and animals.

2. Look through current magazines and books about them (See "Resources.") Then compile a list. Some of the names on your list will probably surprise you.

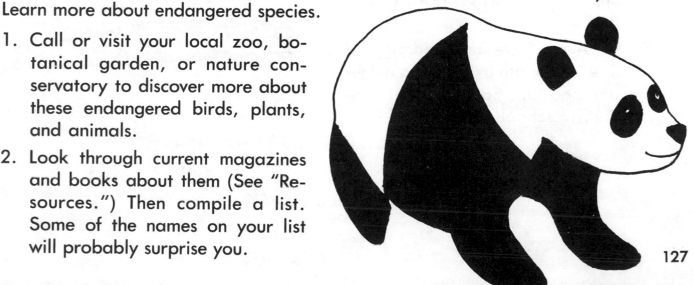

Baby pandas in China (starving from a lack of bamboo to eat)

Baby black rhinoceroses (can grow to 4,000 pounds)

African elephants (being killed for their ivory tusks)

Tapirs (Africa: a shy, solitary animal)

Orangutans (jungles of Borneo and Sumatra)

Ocelots (S. American cat, beautiful fur)

Killer whales

Timber wolves

Sea hawks, spotted owls, and whooping cranes

Piping plovers, harp seals (beautiful white coats)

3. Cut out or draw pictures and make a scrapbook. Tell something about each one, and also what can be done to save them.

4. Make up some matching or board games, a quiz, or crossword puzzle.

5. Plan an exhibit for your school that could include bulletin board displays, stories and news articles, a radio broadcast, a play or puppet show, art projects, and so forth.

6. Have a "Save the Endangered Species" booth as part of a neighborhood fair, Earth Day celebration, or school event.

The Piping Plover

You've probably heard about many of the birds and animals on the Endangered Species list, but did you know about the piping plover? It looks somewhat like a sandpiper, with a small, stocky, sand-colored body. It runs in short steps and stops and often pretends to have a broken wing, to keep away larger birds and predators.

If anything or anyone disturbs the eggs during nesting, the parents will leave the nest and not come back. That's why there are roped-off areas on Atlantic Ocean beaches during the nesting season. Large signs warn beach-goers not to come near so more baby plovers can survive.

SEA AND LAND

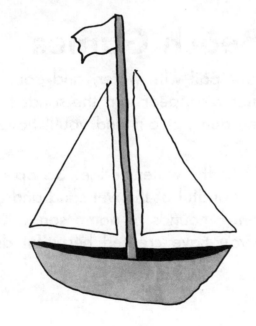

The Sea Shore

Have you ever seen a real ocean? The blue-green water stretches along the shore as far as your eye can see. Sometimes the ocean has light streaks where there are sandbars, or gloomy dark places where there are shadows. Sometimes it is very wavy, other times as calm as a pond. But it always tastes very salty. And, except around our most southern states, it is cold. Do you know why?

In summer the water warms up enough for jumping the waves and swimming. The tide goes in and out twice a day. At low tide you can find lots of shells and sea creatures that have washed up on the sand.

If you are lucky enough to live near a lake or an ocean, or to take a trip there, you'll enjoy trying some of these games and crafts.

Beach Games

1. Dig in the sand, fill your pail with water, and pour it into the holes and tunnels. Watch the water disappear into the sand. Pack some damp sand back into the pail; then dump it out and you'll have the beginnings of a castle or a cake.

2. Make drip castles close to the water's edge. Scoop out a hole until it fills with water. Then take a handful of the wet sand and let it dribble and drip through your fingers onto mounds of damp sand. Keep on dribbling the sand and water until you have created beautiful drip castles around a shallow lake.

Cut the Cake

1. To play Cut the Cake, poke a stick or a feather into a sand cake and take turns carving out slices with your hands.

2. Whoever knocks down the candle has to pay a forfeit (stand on his or her head, run to the water and back three times, find two feathers or a speckled rock, make the cake for the next game). What other forfeits can you think up?

Sand Pictures

1. Smooth off an area of sand with your hands or a shovel (you might want to dampen the sand first), and draw a picture in the sand with a sharp stick or the point of a feather.

2. Write your name, even a note to someone . . . it's almost like having pencil and paper at the beach!

3. To protect your picture or writing, place small rocks and shells all around the outside.

Active Games

1. Mark off an area on the sand and play catch. Then divide it in half. The center line will be the net.

2. Play various games with 1 or more players on each side of the net. Toss a ball or a bean bag, or use your beach towel like a scoop to catch and toss the ball back and forth.

3. Throw a frisbee over the net. Stick a feather in a styrofoam ball and catch it in a bucket, or find some wide sticks to paddle it. Rig up a basket on a stick and play La Crosse.

4. Think up as many games as you can . . . how about Grandmother, May I? or some relay races?

5. Turn your play area into a ball field (you'll need more space), and find something for the bases. Play with a bat and ball, or make up a game where you just run around the bases.

Seagull and Sandpipers

Another beach game that is always fun for a group is called Seagull and Sandpipers, which is similar to Fox and Geese or Cut the Pie, a game usually played in the snow. The players trample a large circle in the sand and then make 3 intersecting paths and a small solid circle in the center, for the safety zone (see illustration).

To play the game, chose someone to be "It," the Seagull, while the others are the Sandpipers. The Seagull stands in the safe zone and at a signal, the Sandpipers run around the paths, trying not to be caught by the Seagull. Whomever is tagged helps the Seagull catch the rest of the Sandpipers. The last one caught becomes "It" for the next game.

If the group is very large, just make the circle larger, or trample 2 circles into the sand for the playing area. You could also start out with 2 or 3 Seagulls, all trying to tag the Sandpipers. Still another variation might be to have the Seagull and the Sandpipers hop, jump, skip, or walk.

Rock Creatures

Go on a rock hunt. Gather rocks of different sizes, colors, and shapes. When you get home, you can sort them all out; then glue some together to make rock creatures. Decorate them with tempera paint and turn them into creatures by

gluing on bits of felt, shells, and smaller rocks to make ears, eyes, tongues, tails, manes, hats, etc. Use the biggest ones as paperweights. Start a rock collection in an egg carton box and see how many different kinds you can find.

Mermaids and Other Sea Creatures

Gather some smooth round or oval rocks. Find beautiful shells and some seaweed (keep it in a plastic bag until you get home). Then paint faces on the rocks, glue on some shells for decoration, and press damp seaweed on for long, flowing hair. When the seaweed dries, it will stick to the rock. Keep your mermaids on display for as long as the seaweed lasts.

Starfish

Find some five-pointed starfish lying on the sand, and take them home in a bucket of water or a plastic bag. Let them soak outdoors in alcohol overnight, or boil them on the stove to get rid of the odor. Let them dry, and they will last for a long time. Press a starfish into a jar lid filled with plaster of paris, and you'll have a lovely plaque.

Display your colorful rocks, shells, starfish, sand dollars, rock creatures, mermaids, and other beach treasures, or use them to decorate picture frames, boxes, and other containers.

Rock Pots

Hunt for large smooth rocks to use as forms for making wonderful clay pots and utensils. Just roll out your clay into a slab, then wrap it halfway around the rock. Cut around it with a dull knife at the widest point of the rock. Turn it over and flatten it to make an even base. Decorate it with a manicure stick, paper clip, or your fingernail. Let the clay harden a little, then loosen the edges. When the clay is firm enough to hold its shape, slip off the pot and allow it to dry for several days. Leave your rock pots as is, paint them, or take them to be fired.

Thanks to Alexis Haas Rubin for helping with these pages

Build an Oceanarium

An exciting project would be to create a model oceanarium for sea animals and plants, similar to the real one now being constructed in Chicago from 1,000 tons of structural steel, 3,250 truckloads of concrete, nine miles of underground pipes, 104 miles of electric cables, and 20,000 square yards of six-inch thick glass. It will take 375 tons of salt compounds and three million gallons of salt water to create Chicago's ocean habitat.

Build your miniature aquarium-oceanarium out of blocks, modeling compound, and saved materials.

YOU NEED:

Large cardboard box lid or a
   tray
Modeling compound

Blocks, chicken wire or mesh, telephone wires, large pan

Sponges, sticks, clay, or fun dough

Tempera or acrylic paint

YOU DO:

1. Use a large box lid or an old tray for creating the ocean/land environment.

2. Construct the aquarium or sea museum out of blocks and cardboard. Put up a flag or banner on the roof with the name.

3. For the round tanks, retaining walls, and sea water of the oceanarium a modeling compound would be the best. Mould it with your hands, or use mesh or chicken wire as a base and form the dough over it. A lift-off domed roof will allow you to play with the sea creatures inside.

4. Model low, rounded areas for trees and bushes and flat spaces for grass, water, people, and boats.

5. Paint your relief map, oceanarium, and sea areas with the appropriate colors. (Leave the blocks plain, if they come from a good set.)

6. Make trees, bushes, people, boats, and fish to put in your scene.

7. You might want to include the same marine or sea animals that the Chicago Oceanarium will have:

   • White-sided dolphins (sometimes called marine acrobats).

   • False killer whales (cousins of the toothed killer whales), who leap high above the water and are strong swimmers.

   • Alaskan sea otters, whose thick fur traps air and keeps them warm. They eat small fish found in kelp or seaweed.

   • Beluga white whales, whose thick layers of blubber keep the cold away. They are sometimes called sea canaries because of their squeals and chirps.

   • Harbor seals, excellent swimmers whose pups are born on ice floes and dive into icy water at two or three days old.

8. Include also the Chambered Nautilus, after which Captain Nero's vehicle is named. This is a large snail-like mollusk with squid-like tentacles, dating back on earth 300 million years. The Nautilus moves slowly along near the bottom of the ocean in the Indo-Pacific islands. Also interesting are sea urchins, round shell-like creatures with a small hole in the top. They resemble Indian pots, or perhaps the pots look like them.

9. There will also be aquatic birds—penguins from the Falkland Islands, whose paddle-like arms and feet help them fly underneath the water at up to 20 miles an hour, although they can't fly through the air.

10. Make some clay sea animals to put in a tidal pool, including anemones, mussels, crabs, surfperch, and sea stars, a better name for starfish. They have no backbone so really are not fish.

ADD-ONS:

Visit your local aquarium, if you can, to find out what kinds of fish can be found in their tanks and window displays. Look in some books and magazines to learn more about aquatic life: plants; fishes; reptiles; invertebrates; amphibians; birds; and marine mammals. (You may have to look some of these words up).

Make a set of Aquarium Cards, similar to Zoo Cards.

Collect shells, rocks, coral, sand, and small weeds to put in your ocean environment.

Be a Nautical Archaeologist

Have you ever wanted to go on an archaeological dig? There are many sites still being excavated where scientists are discovering very old objects or artifacts, such as dinosaur bones, fossils, cave paintings, pottery, and even entire cities beneath the earth.

Today, archaeological digs are also taking place on the bottom of the ocean! This exciting happening is due to the development of special underwater cameras that are powerful enough to reveal ancient shipwrecks that lie miles below the ocean's surface. Nautical archaeologists are diving deep into the water to bring up furnishings, artifacts, and treasures from ships dating back to the 7th century and as recently as the World War II transport ship, *President Coolidge*.

Pretend you are a nautical archaeologist looking for ocean sites filled with treasures from long ago. Write a story, put on a play or puppet show, make a diorama, or gather up some miniature people and props and act out the story.

YOU NEED:

Small plastic people, diving
  gear and other props (tiny
  cameras, spyglasses,
  flashlight, charts, large soft
  brushes, suction hose, ropes,
  nets, chest or box for
  keeping found treasures and
  artifacts: furniture, statues,
  paintings, eating utensils,
  coins, jewels)

A boat (power or sail) for the
  voyage

Sea Creatures

Large map of the world, box
  lid or cardboard

YOU DO:

1. Gather up your crew of miniature people and other things you'll need for the voyage. You might want to use a large map or box lid for your scene (drawing and coloring in the land and the ocean areas) or reenact the expedition on a table or the floor.

2. Chart your voyage ahead of time, marking the general location of the exploration before beginning your underwater adventure.

3. When your ship reaches the area, have your camera crew take underwater pictures to spot the site of a shipwreck. What ancient Spanish ship have you discovered?

4. Next, make preparations to send down the archaeologists (equipped with diving masks, fins, oxygen tubes, and excavating tools) to explore the wreck. What sea creatures will they meet on the way?

5. Once on the ocean's bottom, the real work of excavating the ship will begin. When the wreck is reached, the divers will have to swim around it carefully, so they won't disturb or harm any of the contents. Will they be able to go in and out of the windows and doorways? How will they remove the sand and seaweed from the wreck?

6. The job of bringing up the ship's furnishings, artifacts, and other treasures will be very tricky. You'll have to use waterproof boxes, ropes, chains, and pulleys to hoist everything up to the salvage boat with its anxiously awaiting crew.

7. Now the real archeology will begin! Although most of the actual work—carefully cleaning, putting together the pieces, examining, recording and documenting the found objects—will be done later, your crew will want to photograph and record as much data as they can. Don't forget to have them send out news releases and stories over the ship's fax machine. Everyone will be waiting to hear about your exciting discoveries!

8. After the voyage, all of the items will be taken to an archaeological laboratory or museum where scientists will continue the job of cataloging the contents. What new facts will they learn about life centuries ago?

ADD-ONS:

Before starting the expedition, you may want to read up on this exciting new science at your local library to learn more about ocean life, underwater photography, salvage ships, deep sea diving navigation charts, and Spanish treasure ships. Keep a list of the new words or terms you dig up, and a scrapbook of facts, stories, and pictures. Make a chart of the various wrecks discovered so far.

Compare ocean archaeologists with land ones, noting what is the same about them and what is different. Do you think you might want to be an archaeologist someday?

Mock Volcano

YOU NEED:

Sand, water, ¾ cup vinegar

½ cup dishwashing liquid

Red food coloring

¼ cup baking soda

A large juice can

YOU DO:

1. Mix together 1 cup of water, a few drops of food coloring, the vinegar, and the dishwashing liquid.

2. Make a cone of sand (the sandbox is a good place to do this experiment) and bury the juice can in the center, leaving the open end up and uncovered.

3. Carefully pour the baking soda into the can. Then pour some of your magic mixture in . . . and watch the volcano erupt!

4. Use the remaining mixture to create more eruptions.

5. Look in some science books to discover more about volcanoes.

Note: If you concoct this in your house or garage, be sure to place newspapers underneath, or use a large box lid to contain the sand.

Make a Dinosaur Fossil

The word fossil means hard, stone-like, or rigid. Fossils are the hardened remains of plants or animals. The discovery of dinosaur fossils ten or fifteen years ago in Montana and other places helped scientists or paleontologists learn many new facts about those ancient creatures. They discovered that some dinosaurs behaved more like birds than reptiles, laying eggs and caring for their young in huge nests. You can make model plaster dinosaur eggs, nests, and bone fossils.

YOU NEED:

Sand, plaster of paris

Disposable container, stick

Cardboard or wood strips

Shells, pebbles, sticks, ferns, weeds

Water, sponge

YOU DO:

1. The best place for experimenting with plaster fossils is the beach or a sandbox. However, with care,

you can set up an indoor work area to do this with a minimum of mess.

2. Wet sand with water, and scoop out an area in the sandbox with your hands to serve as a mold; or put wet sand in a large box lid, in plastic or disposable bowls, or on a tray.

3. Place a few natural objects on top of the sand mold. Then mix up the plaster according to the directions on the package, and pour it on top and around each object.

4. Wait about 45 minutes (or less if your objects are small), and your fossils will be hard and stonelike. Lift the plaster fossils from the sand mold, and brush off the sand. Turn the fossils over. What kind did you create? A dinosaur egg or bone, a fern, shell, a lump of coal, or even a cockroach? Or a fossil print of your hand or foot?

5. To make a hand or a foot fossil, press your hand into the plaster, or step quickly in or out of it. Be sure to wash off the plaster immediately, as it might irritate your skin.

6. Carefully wrap your fossils in newspaper or store them in a plastic bag. Display them as part of a nature or dinosaur display, or give them as a gift.

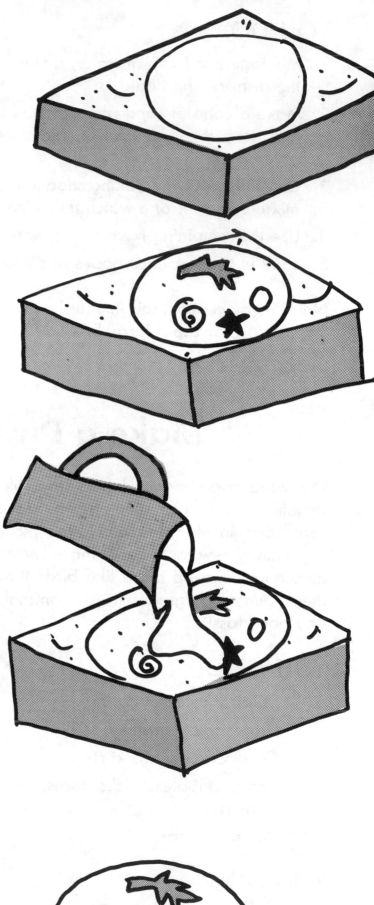

ADD-ONS:

Be careful not to throw any plaster down the sink, as it will clog up the pipes.

To make a dinosaur nest, gather up some straw and other grasses and form them into a nest shape. Pour some plaster over the nest mold, and let it harden. Then you can fill it with plaster or clay eggs, or rounded rocks. The Montana nests were huge (up to 3'–6' long) and the babies were at least 2 ½ times larger than human babies. What materials would be good for creating dinosaur babies and parents?

Make a Montana dinosaur dig diorama in a large carton or shoe box, or a scene in a cardboard lid or tray. Put in hills and mountains, a stream, dinosaurs, nests, eggs, and babies. You might even show the paleontologists on the scene.

Learn more about the new dinosaur discoveries at your library or natural history museum. As you well know, dinosaurs are fascinating creatures!

Fossil Bones and Other Objects

Here's a quick way to make fossilized objects without a lot of mess:

YOU NEED:

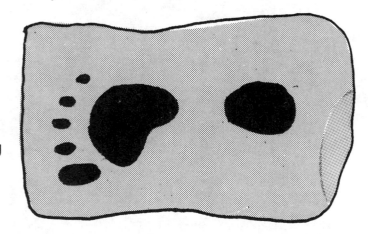

Clay or fun dough

Objects like twigs, rocks, kitchen utensils

Plaster gauze (found at drug stores)

Vaseline, paint (optional)

YOU DO:

1. Decide what kind of fossil you'd like to make: dinosaur bones, eggs, a nest, cooking utensil, your hand or foot.

2. Make the objects out of clay or fun dough, or use real objects.

3. Dampen strips of the plaster gauze and carefully wrap them around the object, making several layers. If you are doing anything that will stick, smear Vaseline on it first (including your hand or foot).

4. Wait a few minutes until the gauze dries and becomes hard. Then remove the object (you may have to cut the gauze a little), and you will have a fossil!

5. Paint or decorate your completed fossil, if you wish, but remember that most bones and fossil pieces are white or a brownish color.

ADD-ONS:

Papier-mâché strips can be used in the same way. These will be lighter in weight and will need painting. Your fossils can be used as a decoration or a paper weight. Grandma would be thrilled to have your hand, foot, or shoe fossil!

Some artists like to make plaster face masks, but this takes great care. George Segal is a famous artist who creates life-sized plaster figures. He always leaves them white.

WHAT'S IN A NAME?

If you are a girl and your first name is Jessica, Jennifer, Amanda, Sarah, or Ashley; or a boy named Matthew, Jonathan, Brian, Michael, or Jason, you have one of the most popular names of the late 1980s.

Names are very special. Do you know how you got your name? Did your parents name you after someone in your family (a grandparent or great aunt)? Or perhaps the date of your birth decided the name—Carol, April or May, Martin (if your birthday is February 15) or George (February 19) . . . or some other famous person.

What were the most common names when your Mom and Dad were children? It's fun to look up names in a book to see where they came from and what they mean. Last names are interesting too. Years ago they came from the person's occupation or where he or she lived. Many names came from the Bible. Today's most frequently encountered names are Johnson, Smith, and Williams. Garcia and Rodriquez are the most common Hispanic surnames. If you could change your name, what ones would you chose?

Name Research

1. Ask your parents and grandparents what the most popular names of their era were.
2. Look in a local phone book or newspapers and magazines to find some unusual names.
3. Search through "Name-Your-Baby" books at the library to find out what your name means.
4. Write down your findings and make a name book. Keep a separate page for your favorite ones, the most unusual ones, ethnic names and their country of origin, made-up names, etc.
5. Many children have *two* last names these days. Children and parents have different last names too, just to add to the confusion. Just remember the old saying, "What's in a name"? It's not the name that's important, it's YOU.

Nicknames

1. If you don't have a nickname, would you like one? Is there something special about you that could turn into a nickname? Your place in the family (Sis or Junior), how you look (Shorty, Fats, or Smiley), or just plain silly names (Boo or Goopers).

2. If you were to make up a nickname, what would it be?

Towns and Counties

If you live in a town or city named Fairview, Midway, Oak Grove, Franklin, Riverside, Centerville, Mount Pleasant, Georgetown, Salem, or Greenwood, you are living in a place whose name is among the ten most frequently encountered ones in the United States. Can you guess where some of these names came from? Seven of them probably were named after something in nature, either an adjective (pleasant, fair, green) or a position or place (Midway, Riverside, Centerville). Two, Georgetown and Franklin, are named after famous Americans. How do you think Salem got its name?

What county do you live in? If it's called Washington, Jefferson, Franklin, Jackson, or Lincoln, then your county has one of the five most often used names in the country. All of these names also have something in common—they are all named for U.S. presidents. Consider these points:

1. It is said that in 1796, two Revolutionary War soldiers came to a town in Pennsylvania and remarked, "Oh, what a fair view!" Fairview, Oregon was named by pioneers in the 1840s who had an outlook post. Fairview,

Kentucky is the birthplace of Civil War hero Jefferson Davis, and has a 300-foot-high monument to him on 22 acres of ground.

2. Midway, the second most popular name, is misleading in most towns, as they aren't midway between anything.

3. The names of other towns are misleading too. Snow Flake, Arizona hasn't any snow at all; Sunshine, Louisiana on the banks of the Mississippi was once called the gloomy name, Forlorn Hope. In May, 1984, during a solar eclipse, the post office there was flooded with letters of people wanting the postmark, "Sunshine."

4. Does your hometown have any interesting stories or facts in its background?

Name Poems

Write a poem about yourself or a friend, using the letters of your name, as in these poems:

Lisa, so lively
Is interested in
Science, swimming, and
Art.

Zachary loves going to the zoo,
After school sports,
Cooking and eating
Hamburgers.
And he is always happy at
Recess time
Year round!

Nicholas is nice,
Isn't he? He loves
Candy and
Holidays,
Oat bran muffins,
Lemon drops and licorice.
And he always has a
Smile!

My Name Is

1. Think up a sentence that tells your name and something about you.

   My name is Andy and I am artistic.

   My name is David and I look daffy.

   My name is Molly and I am marvelous.

2. Change the line by adding how you feel, or where you are going, or what you like to eat, etc.

   My name is Courtney and I feel cute or clever.

   My name is Nicholas and I am going to New York to eat noodles.

   My name is Zachary and I am going to the zoo to see zebras.

Silly Sentences

1. Using the *first letter* of your name, make up a sentence with each word starting with that letter:

   Alexis always arrives alone.

   Sara says silly sayings.

   Ben blows beautiful bubbles.

   Joel jumps just like a jack-in-the-box.

   Lisa loves little lizards.

   Rachel rushes to read the reviews.

2. Try repeating the sentence as fast as you can. If you say your silly sentence swiftly, it will become a tongue-twister!

3. What other name games can you think up?

Name Signs

To mark your favorite possessions (things) or for your room or desk at school, think of some interesting ways to write your name. Design a trademark or logo for yourself!

1. Use cardboard strips or file cards, paper plates, tongue depressors, peel-off labels . . . and some of the ideas below:

2. For lettering, use cut-out newspaper letters, stencils, freehand lettering, tracing, glue and yarn, rice pasta, dots, and sandpaper.

3. Think about shapes: write your name and make a shape out of it. Would it fit in a circle? a triangle? an X?

4. Make a flower and write the letters in the petals.

5. Draw cartoon or stick figures to form the letters of your name.

6. Make name shadow print.

Celebrity Names

Some movie stars and singers are so well known that they can be recognized by only their first name: Ella (Fitzgerald); Frankie (Sinatra); Liza (Minelli); Sammy (Davis), and Elvis (Presley). And some famous stars have only *one* name: Madonna, Cher, Tiffany. Can you think of some more?

OUTDOOR GAMES

Games, games, games . . . children everywhere enjoy playing games. Group games can be played wherever there is space: in your backyard or driveway; at a park or schoolyard; at the beach. All you need is a gang of kids, some rules (or make up your own), and, occasionally, a ball or other equipment.

Besides the well-loved favorites such as Red Rover, Hide-and-Go-Seek, Statues, and Follow the Leader, try some of these games, setting boundaries to limit the playing area.

Giant Chain Tag

The person who is "it" tries to tag each of the other players, one at a time. When a player is caught, he or she loops arms with "it" and then with the others when they are caught, forming a giant chain. After everyone has been connected to the chain, the game starts again, with the first "link" being "it."

Tommy Can't Cross the Sea

All of the players line up on one side of the "sea," and the leader stands across from them on the opposite "shore." The leader calls out, "Tommy can't cross the sea unless his name begins with a B," or "he's wearing green," or "he has curly hair" . . . whatever he or she decides to say.

Whoever has that initial, or is wearing that color, etc., gets to cross the ocean, while all of the others start running towards the shoreline, trying to keep from being tagged. The game continues until all of the players are caught. The last one left is "it" for the next game.

Celebrity Stoop Tag

Whoever is tagged stoops down and quickly calls out the name of a famous person or animal (from a television or radio program, comic strip, book, movie, etc.). If he can't think of a name by the count of three, he becomes "it."

Tricky Dancers

1. This is a game similar to Statues. Everyone dances to the beat of a drum, or other music, going faster and faster without missing a step.

2. When the drum stops, all movement also stops and the dancers freeze.

3. Whoever moves at all, even a small wiggle or a twitch, is out of the game.

4. The game continues until everyone has been tricked and must sit down. Then the music begins again. Who will be able to freeze the longest this time?

5. Other music to try: hand clapping, singing, tambourine, maraca, or a piano, record player, or tape recorder.

ADD-ONS:
Besides dancing, you could skip, hop, jump, twirl, imitate a bird or animal, or whatever else you can dream up.

Have a Ball

There are hundreds of games that can be played with a ball . . . from tiny rubber jacks balls to huge basketballs. Balls come in all sizes, colors, and materials (even a rolled-up sock or a crumpled newspaper will do). Enjoy playing some of these unusual ball games; play some old-timers too, and add more of your own invention.

Stoop Ball

If you don't have space to play a regular game of baseball with bases to run, here's a good substitute. All you need is some steps or a front stoop, a ball, and a few kids to play.

1. The first batter up throws a small, bouncy ball as hard as he or she can at the steps. She scores a hit, if the ball is caught on the first bounce by someone in the field; it's an out, if the ball is caught on the fly.

2. A double is scored if the ball bounces twice before being caught; a triple, if it bounces three times, and a home run if the ball sails all of the way across the yard and over the fence, or into the street.

3. Be sure to keep a sharp eye out for cars when running to retrieve the ball. Keep score just like regular baseball, except no bases are run.

Roof Ball

Children have been playing this game for years, making up their own rules as they go.

1. You need a slanting roof or a wall to play . . . any sized ball will do. Take turns throwing the ball up on the roof and catching it as it rolls down again. Count how many times you can catch it on the fly; then let it bounce once, twice, three times, and so forth.

2. Make up a song or a chant to accompany the action. For example,

Ball, ball, ball on the wall,
How long will it take you to
fall,
   fall,
     fall?
Watch the ball go up,
Watch the ball run down.
Watch the ball circle the roof
  and run all the way down.

Up in Orbit

1. First, make two large circles, with the inner circle of players facing the outer one.

2. The object is to see how long the ball (a beach ball works well) can be kept in orbit (up in the air) before falling to the ground. Try playing this with 1 hand behind your back, or hitting the ball with your head, or any other way you can think up.

3. Have the inner circle of players lie on their backs and kick the ball to the outer players, trying not to let it touch the ground. How long can you keep the ball in orbit this time?

Blanket Ball

1. You will need two blankets or tablecloths and two balls to play this game. Divide into two teams and practice holding onto the edges of the blanket and throwing the ball high in the air, then catching it again.

2. Next, have one team throw the ball up in the air for the other team to catch. You will have to move quickly! Then see if you can throw the ball sideways, back and forth, until one team misses. At a signal each team could throw ball, quickly change places, and catch the other ball.

3. An even harder challenge is to have four players holding on to the corners of the blanket. After the ball is thrown in the air, the players drop the corners, and four other players quickly take their places *before* the ball lands.

4. Make a giant tunnel out of the blanket with players inside holding it up. Then stand back and throw a ball through the tunnel. See how far away you can stand and still get the ball all the way through. Try kicking the ball through or over the tunnel.

Leisure Time

How do you use your leisure time? What do you do when "there's nothing to do"?

1. Think about what you do every day and make a chart, or draw pictures. Are you surprised that there isn't much time to just play?

2. Make a list of the things you'd really like to do . . . if you just had time. Would it be to read a favorite story or go to a movie or an amusement park? Eat some french fries or a chocolate ice-cream cone? Get a new bike, play baseball, go to a water-slide park or to the beach? Or spend an entire day playing Monopoly?

3. Look through old magazines and find some fun things you'd like to do in your spare time, or on a family outing or vacation. Cut them out and make a "Wish I could" book.

4. Daydream a little; then draw pictures of your dreams. Write captions underneath.

5. Create an original poem, story, or puppet show about your favorite things to do. Who will you include? Your friends and family? Or would you like to meet some new people?

6. If you show your pictures and writing to your parents, a grandparent, uncle, or teacher, maybe some of your wishes will come true!

GAMES FROM OTHER COUNTRIES

Get a gang together and play some African tag games, along with other games that children have enjoyed for generations.

Catch the Tail

1. Set the limits of the play area, then divide into teams and form a chain.

2. The last person on each team dangles a scarf or bandana from a pocket or belt.

3. Each team chases the others, with the first player in line trying to grab a "tail."

4. Play this over and over, changing the make-up of the teams, if you wish.

The Big Snake (Da Ga)

1. One player is chosen to be the snake. Whoever the snake catches must join hands and become part of the snake.
2. Then both ends of the snake try to tag other players.
3. The snake grows longer and longer as the game goes on. Who will be the most slippery player and be the last one tagged?

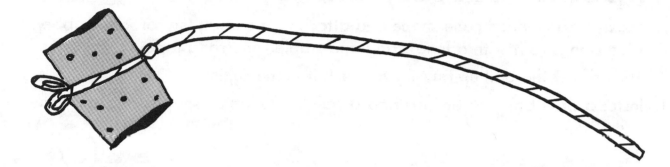

Jumping the Beanbag (Africa)

1. Securely tie a beanbag or rag to a long rope.
2. One person swings the rope low across the ground, while the other players must jump over it or be out of the game.
3. As the circle of jumpers becomes smaller, the rope-swinger makes the rope go faster and faster, until everyone is out.

Chinese Chuck Stone

YOU NEED:

Any number of players, small stones or rocks

YOU DO:

1. Three or more piles of small stones or rocks are placed in a row, about one foot apart.
2. Each player takes a turn and throws a stone at one of the piles, calling out which pile it is.
3. If the player hits the designated pile, he or she keeps one stone from that pile, and gets to throw again.

4. Any scattered stones from the piles remain where they are, becoming targets for future throws.

5. The winner is the player with the most stones, after all of the piles have been removed.

Flipball (Greece, China, and Mexico)

1. Make a cardboard cone shape and attach a small ball (styrofoam, rubber, ping pong) to it with a long string and staples or strong tape.

2. Then throw the ball up and try to catch it in the cup.

3. Instead of a ball, tie on cardboard holiday or other shapes and play the same game.

Chinese Shuttlecock

1. Stick four yellow feathers made from paper or cardboard into a cork.

2. You can only use your heel, toe, or sole of your shoe to kick.

3. See how high and how far you can kick the shuttlecock, or set up a real or pretend net and play with a partner, trying to get the shuttlecock over the net without its touching the ground.

ADD-ONS:
Substitute other materials for the shuttlecock, such as a styrofoam food tray, cardboard, multi-colored construction paper, or real feathers stuck into a small rubber or styrofoam ball. Play the game in your backyard, or on a sidewalk, playground, or beach.

Use paddles to bat the shuttlecock into the air or over the net. If you have lots of players, turn the game into real volley ball with a net and two teams.

Ring and Pin Game

This simple skill game is played in many cultures, including those of the Native Americans. The object is to catch all of the rings on the stick at one time. You could use circles cut from cardboard tubes, curtain rings, bracelets, or canning jar rings. Tie them onto a long string and connect the other end to a stick. Toss the rings up in the air and try to see how many rings you can catch. Will it be one, two, or three?

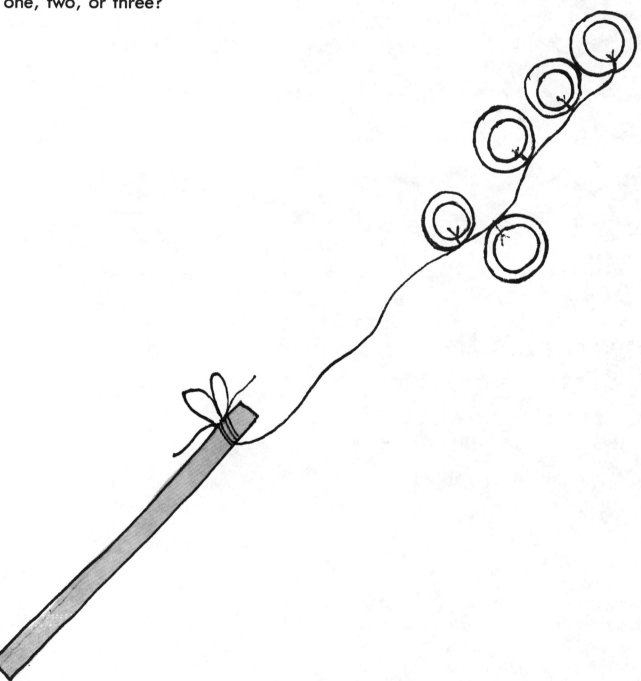

BOARD GAMES AND TIMERS

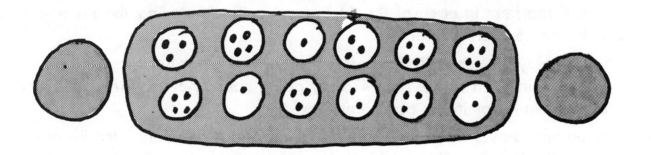

African Kahla or Wari

This is a somewhat complicated but challenging strategy game for two people that dates back thousands of years to Egypt, Asia, and Africa.

YOU NEED:

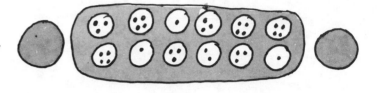

An egg carton and 2 cups

48 counters of markers: seeds, stones, bottle caps, marbles

Marking pens

YOU DO:

1. Mark 1 row of the egg carton A B C D E F and the other one U V W X Y Z. Label the 2 cups "home cup" and place one at either end of the board or egg carton.

2. To play the game, the players pick a row and sit across from each other. Place 4 markers in each of the 6 cups or sections, leaving the home cups empty for "captured" pieces.

3. The first player removes the counters from any of his or her cups and puts or "plants" 1 in each of the next 4 cups, going counter-clockwise. The pieces may land in his or in the opponent's row.

4. The second player does the same thing, moving 4 counters into the next 4 cups to the left, but always skipping over an *empty* cup. If the last counter lands in a cup on the opponent's side that already holds 1 or 2 pieces, the player "captures" the pieces and places them in his or her home cup.

5. Also, that player can remove the counters from the opponent's other cups (to the left) that contain just 2 or 3 pieces.

6. Continue playing the game until all of the compartments on 1 player's side are empty, or until a player can make *no* move at all. In that case, whoever has the most markers in his home cup is the winner.

ADD-ONS:

Try creating a Wari game out of clay, as the ancient players did. You could also make one with cardboard and paper cups, or if you have a home woodworking shop, you could make a handsome one out of wood.

Nine Men's Morris

This traditional, and tricky, board game goes back to the ancient Egyptians! Archaeologists found the game carved into the roof of a temple dated 1400 B.C. Many versions of the game are around, but here is the basic one, adapted from a book of magic. Enjoy creating and playing it with a friend.

YOU NEED:

Cardboard or a large box lid

9 markers for each player
(coins, disks, bottle caps)

Marking pens, ruler, scissors

YOU DO:

1. Draw the board to look like the one in the illustration. It is like a maze with 3 rectangles.

2. Each player has 9 markers of 1 color or kind. Players take turns placing a marker on any vacant circle. Turns are taken by moving 1 marker 1 step, to the next circle.

3. The object of the game is to get 3 in a row of 1 color. When this happens, it is called a "mill." Whoever gets a mill can remove one of the opponent's markers from the game. But no one can take a marker from an opponent's mill unless there is no other marker to take.

4. A mill may be "opened" by moving 1 of the 3 markers off the line, and "closed" by returning it to its former position on the next play.

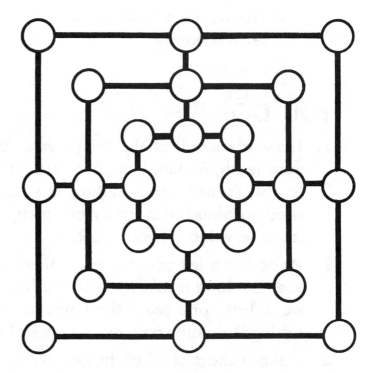

5. The game is won when a player reduces his opponent to only 2 markers or blocks the other player so he cannot move at all.

6. Play this game over and over until you become familiar with all of the strategic moves. What other games does it remind you of?

ADD-ONS:

For a more permanent Nine Men's Morris game, try making one out of wood. This would also make a wonderful gift for a friend. You might want to make a checkers, chess, or tic-tac-toe board out of wood.

Adapted from the *Metropolitan Museum of Art Activity Book* by Osa Brown.

Stopwatch Fun

YOU NEED:

A stopwatch or a watch with a second hand

Objects to time

YOU DO:

1. Think about all of the things you do every day that take time—brushing your teeth, making your bed, eating breakfast, walking to the school bus or to the corner store, setting the table, picking up your toys and books, reading aloud as a family or quietly in your room, watching television or a favorite video on your VCR.

2. Write out a list of activities to time. Then set your stopwatch on "start" and see how long it takes you to finish each item. Try it again the next day or a week later and see if the times are the same. Did it take longer to set the table? Did you watch more or less TV?

3. Make a chart of all of the activities you timed. Check again in a few weeks. What new everyday things can you add? Ask a friend to do the same thing (or a brother or sister), and compare the results. Did you spend more or less time on fun things, chores, health routines?

4. Play some stopwatch games:

   • Look in the mirror and see how long you can stare straight ahead without blinking.

   • How long can you keep silent in the car, hold your breath, or stand on your head?

   • Have a race to see who can put away the groceries the fastest, or pick up the blocks, cars, and animals.

- How long does it take to get a haircut, ride your bike to school, put away the dishes?

What other stopwatch games can you play?

5. Listen to commercials on the radio and on TV . . . time them. Are they 30 seconds, 1 minute, or longer? Are the shorter ones snappier than the longer ones? Which do you remember best?

6. Look in the newspaper at the Sports Section and see if you can find times for a baseball, football, or hockey game, for horse and auto races, a swim meet, or some other sporting event. Go to the library and find a recent *World Almanac*. It will have fastest times for all kinds of events. *The Guinness Book of World Records* has lots of fascinating facts having to do with time.

Where else would you use a stopwatch? Running a race, playing a board game, swimming a length of the pool, eating an ice-cream cone? The list is endless. You might enjoy reading the book *The Stop Watch*, by David Lloyd.

Homemade Timers

Here are some fun and easy ways to make some timers to use while playing board games or taking part in short events or races. Which of these 3-minute timers do you think will be the most accurate? You might want to choose just one, or if you are really ambitious, try all of them. Then you can test them out and see.

Bottle-Up

YOU NEED:

2 plastic soft drink bottles (16-ounce size is good)

A nail, hammer, tape

Salt or clean sand

Markers, contact paper, paint

YOU DO:

1. Wash and dry the bottles and caps. Hammer a nail through the middle of each cap to make holes, and tape the caps together, top sides down.

2. Decorate the bottles, if you wish, with contact paper, markers, or acrylic paint.

3. Fill one of the bottles ¾ full with salt or sand; then screw on the cap. Place the second bottle upside-down onto the top cap and screw it on too. Turn the timer over and the sand or salt will slowly pour from the top to the bottom.

4. To determine how much time it takes for the salt or sand to run from the top bottle into the bottom one, use a stopwatch or a watch with a second hand. To make a 3-minute timer, remove the sand that remains in the top bottle after 3 minutes. Or you may need to add sand if it runs out too fast.

5. Consider making your timer a 1-minute or 2-minute one, if that is closer to the time it takes the salt or sand to run through. You may have to go back and forth several times, adding or removing sand, to calibrate your timer.

6. How will you use your timer? For making soft-boiled eggs, seeing how long it takes to run a short errand or do a chore, or for a guessing game or quiz, or at the telephone so no one in the family talks too long?

For events that take longer, you will have to use a larger timer or a stopwatch.

Simple Water Timer

YOU NEED:

An empty milk carton

Ball point or marking pen, ruler

Water

168

YOU DO:

1. Open the top of the carton, and cut it off so it will be level. Then place a ruler inside and measure off the inches.

2. Poke a small hole at the bottom 2" line.

3. Fill the carton with water and watch the water run through (be sure to work over a sink or a large pan). Time how long it takes for the water to run out.

4. Fill it up to 3" and see how long that takes to drain. Then fill it up again and time how long each inch of water takes to run out. Does it take more or less time per inch as it drains? How accurate do you think this kind of timer is?

Water Timer Extravaganza

YOU NEED:

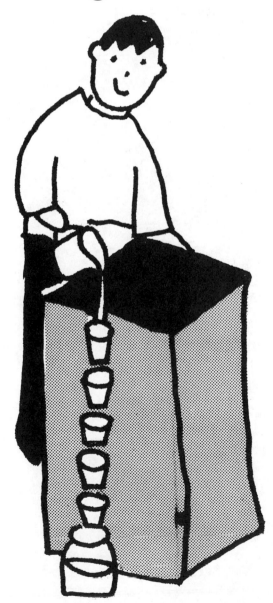

A cardboard box or carton

5 identical styrofoam cups

Brad paper fasteners, nail or ice pick (use with care)

Rocks or books

A glass or plastic jar

Water

YOU DO:

1. With the nail or pick, poke a hole in the bottom of each of the paper cups and 5 holes through the side of the carton. Then fasten the cups with the brads one above the other to the outside of a cardboard carton, as shown in illustration.

2. Weight down the carton with something heavy (rocks or books) to keep it steady. Place an empty jar under the cups to catch the water.

3. Measure and pour 1 cup of water into the top cup of the carton and time how long it takes the water to run through each of the cups and into the jar. Do this again and find out the time it takes for the water to go from one cup to another.

Is this kind of timer more or less accurate than your other one?

ADD-ONS:

Change the time by using fewer or more cups. Turn your water timer into a marble race by enlarging the holes. Decorate the carton if you wish.

Consult the *Smithsonian® Family Learning Activities Science Calendars* for more fun ideas.

NEW IN THE 1990s

From 1890 to 1990

Did you ever stop to think about all of the wonderful inventions that make life comfortable and easy for us? American children of a hundred years ago didn't know about airplanes, escalators, yogurt, or air conditioners.

Play an invention game by finding out when your parents were born. If it was after 1945, then there is a long list of everyday things that both you, and they, probably take for granted. You might be quite surprised at most of the items on the list; even your parents may be surprised.

Before 1945, people didn't have television, microwave ovens, frisbees, or ballpoint pens. There was no such thing as electric blankets. Dishes had to be washed by hand, and summer nights were sweltering without air conditioning. Scientists hadn't invented plastic, laser beams, or contact lenses; there were no FM-radios, tape decks, electric typewriters, or word processors. Freezers and frozen foods weren't around for a quick meal. Everything was paid for with cash or check, because no one had thought up a credit card yet.

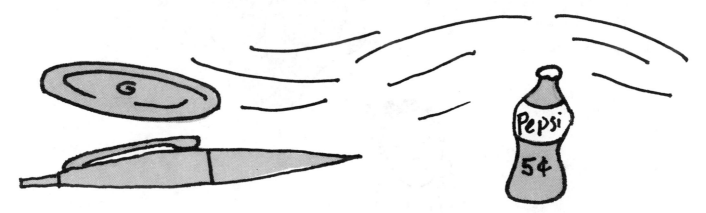

Man hadn't walked on the moon, dime stores really sold things for five and ten cents, gas cost only 11 cents a gallon, and for five cents you could get a Pepsi, send a letter, take a street car, or make a phone call. But you couldn't buy yogurt at any price, because in this country there was no such thing.

After you have looked over this list, ask your friends and family to answer some questions.

1. Which of these things would you miss the most?
2. What other innovations can you list?
3. How much do we pay now for soda pop, a letter, or a phone call?
4. How do you keep cool in very hot weather without an air conditioner?

PLAY A GAME:

1. Find or draw pictures of these inventions, and make invention cards and a board.

2. Use them to play a lotto or a memory game.

3. Tell or write an invention story. Do a picture story.

4. Read up on one or two of the inventions; then put on a play or a radio or TV program. Do a pretend interview with an inventor.

5. Write a story about the olden days before TV, FM-radios, dishwashers, and drip-dry clothes.

BE AN INVENTOR!

What kind of gadget, machine, food, or health aid could you think up to make life even better in the 1990s?

Thanks to Cissy Haas and a newspaper story about a KMPC Los Angeles radio program for this information.

The Year 2040

Forty years ago George Orwell wrote a book called *1984*. In it he predicted what the world would be like in that year. Luckily, his predictions didn't come true, for he said that "Big Brother" would be watching and eavesdropping on everyone, making life very unpleasant.

You might like to predict what the world will be like 40 or 50 years from now. Save your thoughts in a safe place until the year 2040 and see if anything you predicted really came true!

YOU DO:

1. Think about what life will be like 40 or 50 years from today. Will people be living on the moon or on Mars? Will everyone work just three or four days a week and play the rest of the time? Will our food be so nourishing and pure that we can eat whatever we like without worry about our health or getting too fat?

2. Make a list of your predictions. Illustrate your list, if you wish.

3. Write stories about various things on your list and bind them into a book. For example, you might write about:
   • Life in Space
   • Television and Movies
   • School Subjects Children Will Study
   • Leisure or Free Time
   • Winning Sports Teams
   • Once Endangered Species
   • Favorite Foods
   • Favorite songs and music groups

4. Make up a play about your predictions. Plan characters, costumes, scenery, props, and situations for the future.

5. Make a time capsule out of a metal box or tube. Place in it pictures, newspaper clippings, your lists, and stories about the happenings of the current year or season. Then bury your capsule in your backyard or somewhere on your school grounds, or hide it in your basement, attic, or garage. Draw a map showing the location and put it in a safe place. Then in six months or a year, you can dig up your time capsule and remember what you were doing way back then. Invite your friends to share the memories with you.

6. Dream up a 2040 board game. What places will you visit in the game? How will you get there? What will the game markers look like? What will the dangers be? The new adventures and surprises? Enjoy this visit to the future!

Be an Inventor

Is there something new under the sun? The answer is yes. Thousands of new products are invented every year. Can you think up something that could make life more fun or easier? Many others before you have thought that they could, and after tinkering and experimenting in kitchen labs and garage or basement shops for months and even years, have managed to invent something new.

Did you know that almost one quarter of the more than 70,000 patents granted each year by the U.S. Patent Office are issued to home inventors? In fact, it was an 18-year-old boy who, after working for two years and doing 60 designs, invented an important fuel-saving device for airplanes. And a high school girl who, wishing she could write in the dark, recently invented the "Glo-Board." When you place a piece of paper over the board, which is covered with glow-in-the-dark paint, the glow shines through and lets you see to write.

You can make a glow-in-the dark clipboard that will help you write in dark places too.

1. Place a rectangle of cardboard on some newspapers and cover it with glow-in-the-dark or fluorescent paint (available at craft shops).
2. Let it dry. Then poke a hole in the top right-hand corner and attach a long string tied to a pencil or pen.
3. Put a large clip on the top of the board, to hold your paper. Now you're all set for your "after hours" writing.

ADD-ONS:

For added fun, take your glow-in-the-dark clipboard with you to the movies or your backyard or neighborhood clubhouse, or when traveling in a car or a bus, train, or plane at night.

Make miniature glow-in-the-dark boards to give as gifts to your friends. Use acrylic paint or colorful stickers to make decorative borders.

A Century of Telephones

The telephone is an indispensable invention of the 20th century. Telephones are capable of carrying the human voice over great distances—all around the world, in fact! Make a collection of model telephones to display or play with. Start with two cups attached with a long wire, string, or nylon thread. Add an old-fashioned upright phone, a dial phone, a streamlined touch-tone model, a transparent high-tech phone, and finally, a mini-mobile phone. Have a telephone exhibit and invite your friends to contribute to the dazzling display!

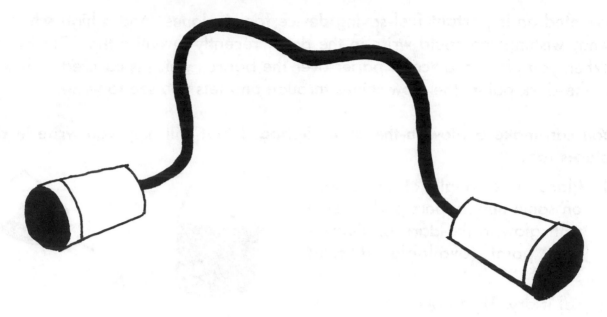

Old-fashioned Upright Telephone

In your great grandpa's day, everyone used a black upright phone and talked directly to an operator when placing a call. Party lines were common then, as was the friendly voice of the operator asking, "What number, please?"

YOU NEED:

A round cardboard lid or styrofoam block

Paper towel and toilet tissue tubes

Paper cups or egg carton cups, small plastic margarine tub with lid

Brads, pipe cleaners, string or yarn

Scissors, glue, black paint

YOU DO:

1. Use the lid of the margarine tub or a circle of styrofoam for the base.

2. Attach the towel tube to the base and glue on the margarine tub and a small cup for the mouthpiece, as in illustration.

3. Fashion a receiver from a toilet paper tube and a paper cup or egg carton section, and tie on string or yarn for the telephone cord.

4. Rig up a holder for the receiver by bending pipe cleaners into a circle, or cutting a half-circle from another tube. Attach it with glue or a brad near the top of the towel tube.

5. For an authentic look, paint your old-fashioned phone black.

6. When you lift the receiver on this phone, imagine that a cheery operator comes on to take your call.

Dial Phone

YOU NEED:

Cardboard box or a mushroom or berry basket

1 long and 1 short cardboard tube

2 small paper cups or egg carton sections

Brads, cardboard, string or yarn

Scissors, glue, markers

Construction and contact paper (optional)

YOU DO:

1. To make a base for your phone, use a box or turn a berry basket upside down.

2. Cut the short tube in half lengthwise and glue it onto the base, for the cradle.

3. For the receiver, attach a cup or egg carton section to each end of the long tube. Tie on a yarn or string cord.

4. To make the dial, cut a circle of cardboard and draw 10 small circles on it with the numbers 1—0 inside, as shown in illustration. Write your own phone number across the middle. (For a more realistic dial, use 2 cardboard circles with the small circles cut out of the top one.) Attach the dial to the base with a brad and your phone is ready for use.

5. Decorate the base and receiver with contact or construction paper ahead of time, if you wish.

Touch-Tone Telephone

YOU NEED:

Shoe box, long thin box like a jewelry or necktie box

Cardboard tube, small paper cups

Sponges, file card

Yarn or string, pipe cleaner

Scissors, glue, markers

YOU DO:

1. Use the shoe box for the base of your phone.

2. Cut out and glue on 12 small sponge squares for the keys. Write the numbers 0–9, plus * and #, on white cardboard and glue each one onto the keys in the correct order.

3. To make the receiver, use the long box, or attach a paper cup to each end of a towel tube. Twist a pipe cleaner and stick it next to the dialing pad as a holder for the receiver.

4. Attach a yarn or string cord, and your push-button phone is ready to be used or displayed.

ADD-ONS:

For variety, you could decorate your phone in bright colors or wild designs, add a memory dial, pad and pencil, and so forth.

High-Tech Transparent Telephone

Today's telephones have joined the high-tech age, with clear plastic see-through versions whose inner workings whirl and light up when the phone rings. Here's how to make a wacky telephone sculpture or model for school or your bedroom.

YOU NEED:

A squat, fat, unbreakable jar or plastic box

Cardboard tubes from toilet paper or paper towels or a tall, thin plastic jar

An old discarded telephone

Telephone wires, colored pipe cleaners

Paint in bright colors, colored cellophane

Foam or sponges

Scissors, glue, glitter, markers

YOU DO:

1. Stuff colored telephone wires, pipe cleaners, small blocks, marbles, some jingle bells—anything that you think looks like the inner workings of a telephone—inside the large jar. (If you are lucky enough to have an old phone, use parts from that).

2. Rig up a receiver from the thin plastic jar or a paper towel tube. Draw an exotic flower, a snake, tiger stripes, a candy stick . . . or whatever you'd like on the tube; or decorate a strip of paper to go inside the plastic jar.

Mini-mobile Phone

Something new has been added to telephones—a tiny mobile model that is about the size of a checkbook and weighs less than a pound. You can make a pocket-sized mobile phone too.

YOU NEED:

A small, thin box with a lid

Cellophane, plastic wrap, or acetate

Knitting needle or dowel

Cardboard, small buttons

Construction or contact paper

Scissors, glue, tape, marker

YOU DO:

1. Use the box for the phone base. Cut a round hole in the top half of the lid for the amplifier. Glue a piece of cellophane or plastic over the opening on the bottom side of the lid.

2. Cover the lid and box with contact or construction paper, or leave it plain.

3. The bottom half of the lid is where the dial goes. Glue on 3 or 4 rows of tiny buttons or cardboard circles with numbers.

4. Finally, stick in a dowel or knitting needle as an antenna, and your mobile phone is all set to go!

Solar Energy

Solar Heat Box

Think about how hot you get in the summertime without air conditioning. The car's hot; your room is, too. Wouldn't it be great to capture all that heat in winter! You can make a solar collector that will capture and store some heat.

YOU NEED:

A cereal, shoe, or shirt box

Sheet of acetate or plastic wrap

Black paint, an old slate, or construction paper

Scissors, paint

Thermometer, watch or timer (optional)

YOU DO:

1. Make a window by cutting out the center of a cereal box or a box lid, leaving about a ½" border.

2. Slide a piece of black construction paper or an old black chalk board inside, or paint the side facing the opening black.

3. Cover the window with a sheet of acetate or plastic wrap and seal it around the edges with tape. (Also seal the flap of a cereal box.)

4. Place your heating box in a sunny spot with the acetate window facing the sun. Wait a little while. Soon, when you put your hand on the box, you will feel some solar heat. This will happen even on a cool day, as long as the sun is shining.

5. Leave your solar heater or absorber in the sun for a longer time. Now when you feel the box, it will be even hotter. You might try putting a thermometer inside to see exactly how hot the trapped air got. How long does it take the air to cool off when you take the box away from the window?

ADD-ONS:

Try using your solar box to make crayon-melt pictures. After the box is heated up, place a piece of paper on top of it and sprinkle some crayon bits across it. Watch what happens. You could try to melt a chocolate bar on it by putting the chocolate on some aluminum foil and then on top of the box.

Some people use solar energy to heat their houses and their water. If you were to make a very large solar heater, as big as a picture window for your house, and placed pipes inside for water to run through, you could heat your bath and sink water.

Solar panels made of photo-electric materials can generate electricity when exposed to the sun. This electricity can run a pocket calculator or even a television set, or charge batteries for electric lights.

Thanks to Larry Clampitt
for helping with this idea.

Solar Water Warmer

Wouldn't it be nice to have a supply of warm water handy when you are playing outside or having a picnic in a park or campground? Here's an easy water container to make and hang up near your campsite. Poke a hole near the bottom of a large plastic bottle, push a plug (a cork or small stick) in the hole, and fill it with water. Let the sun warm it for several hours. Then hold a paper cup or washcloth underneath the spout, pull out the plug, and warm water will slowly trickle out.

If you want to make your water warmer even better, paint the container black with bubble paint, which will stick to the surface better than tempera paint alone. Or glue on black construction paper.

Solar Cooker

Soon solar cooking will be in fashion. On a hot sunny day you won't have to build an outdoor fire for your picnic or barbecue. Just rig up a solar hot dog cooker like this one. Cut a round cardboard oatmeal or grits carton in half, lengthwise. Cover it with aluminum foil and poke a hole through both ends. Then insert two wires (coat hangers work well) for holding the hot dog. Turn the handle as the reflected rays of the sun begin cooking the hot dog. Before long, your food will be ready to eat! Think up other kinds of solar cookers or ovens to make, and other picnic foods for you and your friends to enjoy.

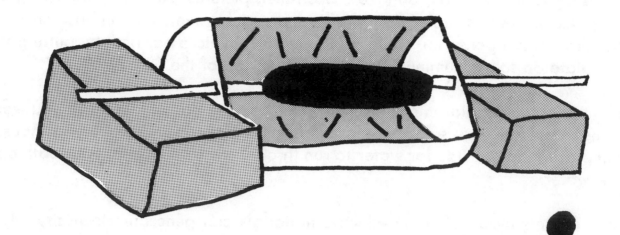

TV's 50th Birthday

Happy 50th birthday to television! It was on April 30, 1937 at the New York World's Fair that the first TV broadcast went on the air. What do you think was the very first image to be projected on the RCA TRK screen? Answer: Felix the Cat!

Soon, your grandparents began squinting at tiny seven-inch television sets housed in large wooden cabinets, laughing at Milton Berle, Jack Benny, Lucille Ball, and Jackie Gleason. In the 1950s, your parents sat glued to "Kukla, Fran and Ollie," "Ding Dong School," "Romper Room," and "Captain Kangaroo."

What are your favorite TV programs?

1. Make a list of your favorite shows; then compare it with your parents' and grandparents' favorites.

2. Play a lotto or matching game. Write your favorite programs on one set of index cards and the name of the people or actors on the other set. Younger children could guess the names from picture cards.

3. Pretend to be a favorite TV character. Put the cards in a drawstring bag or a hat, and let each person pull one out. Try to guess who it is. If no one can guess from your pantomimes, give hints or answer "yes" or "no" to questions.

ADD-ONS:

Younger children will enjoy having parents or older viewers on hand to answer questions or explain difficult or hard-to-understand concepts . . . or just for the sociability. Busy children will be happy to have their favorite programs and specials taped. Then everyone can watch four-star programs over and over!

"Reading Rainbow," and other book-related programs, are a TV must. Consult your newspapers or TV Guides for enrichment programs that turn television into a learning tool, unlocking new doors of knowledge.

Inside TV

Do you notice other things going on in a TV program besides the story? How about the music, the movement, color, light, and dialogue? You might want to jot down notes about the production values of a program, as you watch. Then you could make a chart showing your findings.

1. Do you hear music in the background? Is it soft, loud, peppy, somber, spooky, lighthearted? Do you recognize it? Can you name it and/or the composer?

2. Does the action take place in one room, several places, outside, on a farm, in space, riding in a car or boat? Are the people just sitting or doing something and moving around? Do they mostly talk? What is the background scene like? If it is a sports program, you won't have any trouble with this question.

3. How is the program lighted? Is it shot indoors or outside? Real light, or artificial? Bright or darkish? What kind of light do you usually see at a play or a circus?

4. Does the program use "canned" laughter? Does this help or distract you? Listen to hear if anyone talks with an accent. Can you understand all of the words? Try turning off the sound and figuring out what is said. Pretend to be watching with someone who is deaf or hearing impaired. Explain what is happening and make up some conversations.

Be a TV Script Writer

Sometimes events are recorded on television before they are ever written down. Then we are witnessing history in the making. Most times, however, newscasters write their stories before they present them on TV. You can try your hand at writing a television (or radio) news report, too.

1. Think up a news event, weather forecast, or sports story and write it down on paper.

2. To get ideas, turn on your TV and listen carefully to the person who is talking (the announcer) and to what is being said. Some programs have a "voice-over" to go along with the picture you see on the screen.

3. You will notice that news stories are quite short, especially if they are repeated on a second newscast. Human interest or follow-up stories are longer. The script will look something like this.

Commentator: Good evening. Here is today's top story. Elephant tusks were burned in Africa again, by environmentalists who don't want poachers to kill the elephants for their valuable ivory tusks.

(Camera pans to pictures of elephants and a huge pile of tusks being burned.)

Commentator: Our African correspondent, Roberto Evansky, is on the scene. Roberto. . . .

Correspondent Evansky: Everything is very tense in Kenya tonight.

4. Be sure to leave room on your script for commercials. You might want to time some of the ads, to discover how many there are and how long they run (15, 30, or 60 seconds, usually). Will you write a jingle or a song, or show a people-situation, pet, or picture-story?

5. Ask your parents, aunts, uncles, and grandparents what their favorite commercials of the past are. Will it be "Snap, Crackle, Pop," "J-E-L-L-O," or "See the USA in your Chevrolet," "We are the men of Texaco," or "Dumplings and marshmallowed meatballs?" What are your favorites?

Compose a Commercial

1. Find a product that you like (a cereal, running shoe, cookie, vitamin, toy) and write down all of the things that are special about it.

2. Then draw a picture of the product and print the slogan or description near the drawing. Use the commercial as part of your television script. Make a story board, as the advertising agencies do for their clients. These are a series of sketches, with the script written underneath, that show what happens in the commercial.

3. You might want to make a book of ads for TV, radio, magazines, and newspapers.

4. Create a game by writing slogans on index cards and see if your friends can guess what the products are. Or draw or glue on a picture, and see who can remember the matching slogan. Use the cards to play a memory or lotto game. What other games can you think up?

5. The most fun of all is to make up a new product, design the label and packaging, dream up a zippy slogan, and create a good advertising campaign. Where and how will you show or market your new product? In print (newspapers and magazines), on the air (radio and TV), at a movie theater, or even on a giant billboard? Sometimes names of products are written on long banners and flown from an airplane!

TV Games

Did you know that 99% of all families in the United States own a television set? It's very tempting to turn on the tube when you are bored and have nothing to do, but too much TV watching might turn you into a "couch-potato-kid," something nobody wants to be.

There's a bright side to TV too: it can teach, inspire, entertain, motivate, and enlighten.

Here are some television games you can play to make your TV watching more enjoyable and help you learn, too.

1. What are your favorite sit-coms or TV families? Make a list of them and write a short story about each one. Compare the families—how do they spend their time, work, play, eat? Do they ever disagree or fight? Are they like your family? Do you wish you lived with them? What kinds of things do they do that you also do, or would like to do?

2. Have you seen a good special lately—a holiday cartoon, nature documentary, or science program? Perhaps a program about another country? What did you like about it? How did it make you feel? What new things did you learn?

3. Keep a TV diary: write down every program you watch for a week or a month. Rate the programs 1, 2, 3, 4, 5 or excellent, good, fair, poor. Count up how many hours you watched. Write a short description about each one. Exchange diaries with your friends.

4. Be a television columnist or critic for a magazine or newspaper. Write reports about the programs you would recommend. Give each one a rating, as TV critics do (* * * * for rave reviews). Start a TV column for your school or neighborhood paper, or pretend to be a radio or TV announcer, with a microphone and script.

5. What other ideas do you have about getting the most from TV?

HDTV Set

The 1990s promise to be innovative and exciting for television viewing with the advent of HDTV, or high definition television. The picture is sharper and easier to see, and the sound is better too. Some sets will even cover an entire wall in your home or school! It will be almost like having your own movie theatre.

Make your own HDTV set and write and illustrate an original TV program to show your friends and family.

YOU NEED:

A carton or shoe box

Spools, large buttons, wire hanger

Roll of shelf paper

2 dowels, pencils, or paper towel tubes

Crayons, markers, construction paper

Magazines and newspapers

X-Acto knife, scissors, tape, glue

YOU DO:

1. Cut a large rectangle out of one side of the box or carton, leaving a 2" or 3" frame. Make the screen much longer than wide. (You may need to ask an adult to help you.)

2. Next, cut 2 long slits on each side for the television roll to go through.

3. Add knobs, dials, and a wire hanger antenna, to look like a real set.

4. Think of your favorite television programs; then write a script—a newscast, human interest story, cartoon, sit-com, nature special, or cooking program—and write it down on sections of the paper roll. Measure the screen first to determine the size of each segment. Then illustrate your story. (Younger children could just draw pictures and/or dictate words and sentences to someone older.)

5. Attach the last section of your completed program to one of the dowels or cardboard tubes, and roll it up, leaving the front end to thread through both slits. Glue the loose end to the other roller. You might want to rig up some kind of a holder to keep the rolled paper next to the sides of the carton.

6. Now you're all set for the premiere showing of your television show! Gather up your audience, and turn on the set. Slowly unroll the pictures from left to right, narrating as you go.

Video-Letter Booth

Did you ever have your picture taken in a dime-store photo booth? For about one dollar you can get three or four small pictures of yourself mugging in front of an instant camera. There are photo booths all over the United States, and in over 100 foreign countries.

Now you can tape a 10-minute video letter in a Video-Letter Booth. Dreamed up by a California inventor in 1988 and produced a year later by a company aptly called "Short Takes," video cassette letters are a reality. For a five-dollar bill and three one-dollar bills, you can sit in a booth, press a red button, and start speaking! A moving backdrop will be behind you (there are several choices) to liven up the video.

Video letters would make a great gift for Mom and Dad, a faraway grandparent, aunt, or friend. Sick in bed and missed an assignment? Read your story or report in front of the video recorder and you'll probably get an A! Applying for a job? Sell yourself with video. As time goes by, people will think up lots of reasons to visit a video booth.

Resources

Arts and Crafts

Allen, Janet. *Exciting Things To Do with Nature Materials.* Philadelphia: J. B. Lippincott Co., 1977.

Arnold, Arnold. *The Complete Book of Arts and Crafts for Children.* New York: Thomas Y. Crowell, 1975.

Arnosky, Jim. *Sketching Outdoors in Spring.* New York: Lothrop, Lee & Shepard Books, 1986.

Bernstein, Bonnie, and Leigh Blair. *Native American Crafts.* Belmont, CA: David S. Lake Publishers, 1982.

Brown, Osa. *Metropolitan Museum of Art Activity Book.* New York: Harry N. Abrams, 1983.

Burns, Marilyn. *Good Times: Everykid's Book of Things To Do.* New York: Bantam Books, 1979.

Butterfield, Moira, and Susan Peach. *Usborne Guide to Photography.* London: Usborne Publishing Ltd., 1987.

Curtis, Annabelle, and Judy Hindley. *The Know How Book of Paper Fun.* London: Usborne Publishing Ltd., 1975.

Edwards, Betty. *Drawing on the Right Side of the Brain.* Los Angeles: Jeremy P. Tarcher, 1979.

Garritson, Jane. *Child Arts.* Reading, MA: Addison-Wesley Publishing Co., 1979.

Gibbons, Gail. *The Pottery Place.* New York: Harcourt Brace Jovanovich, 1987.

Grater, Michael G. *Creative Paper Toys and Crafts.* New York: Dover Publications, 1981.

Horn, George. *Art for Today's Schools.* Worcester, MA: Davis Publications, 1975.

Irvine, Joan. *How To Make Pop-Ups.* New York: William Morrow & Co., 1987.

Kinser, Charleen. *Outdoor Art for Kids.* Crystal Lake, IL: Follett Library Book Company, 1975.

Kohl, Mary Ann. *Mudworks, Creative Clay, Dough, and Modeling Experiences.* Bellingham, WA: Bright Ring Publishing, 1989.

————. *Scribble Cookies: And Other Independent Creative Art Experiences for Children.* Bellingham, WA: Bright Ring Publishing, 1989.

Lawler, Tony. *Beginners Guide to Woodwork.* London: Usborne Publishing Ltd., 1979.

Lucie-Smith, Edward. *The Thames and Hudson Dictionary of Art Terms.* London: Thames and Hudson Ltd., 1984.

Michalski, Ute, and Tilman Michalski. *Windcrafts.* Chicago: Childrens Press, 1990.

Murray, William, and Francis J. Rigney. *Paper Folding for Beginners.* New York: Dover Publications, 1960.

Newsome, Arden. *Craft Toys from Around the World.* New York: Julian Messner, 1972.

Nicklesburg, Janet. *Nature Crafts for Early Childhood.* Reading, MA: Addison-Wesley Publishing Co., 1976.

Pearson, Tracey Campbell. *Dollhouse People.* New York: Viking Kestrel, 1984.

Rasmussen, Richard, and Ronda Lea Rasmussen. *The Kid's Encyclopedia of Things To Make and Do.* St. Paul, MN: Toys 'n' Things Press, 1981.

Reid, Barbara. *Playing with Plasticine.* New York: William Morrow & Co., 1988.

Simons, Robin. *Recyclopedia.* Boston: Houghton Mifflin Co., 1976.

Thompson, David T. *Easy Woodstuff for Kids.* Mount Ranier, MD: Gryphon House, 1981.

Walker, Lester. *Carpentry for Children: Plans for Great Do-It-Yourself.* New York: The Overlook Press, 1985.

Wankleman, Wigg. *A Handbook of Arts and Crafts.* Dubuque, IA: William C. Brown Group, 1972.

Weil, Lisl. *Let's Go to the Museum.* New York: Holiday House, 1989.

Weiss, Harvey. *Beginning Artist's Library.* Reading, MA: Addison-Wesley Publishing Co., 1978.

Wilkes, Angela. *My First Activity Book.* New York: Alfred A. Knopf, 1990.

Wilms, Liz, and Dick Wilms. *Exploring Art.* Elgin, IL: Building Blocks, 1986.

Wiseman, Ann. *Making Things: Book 2.* Boston: Little, Brown & Co., 1975.

Wurmfeld, Hope. *Boatbuilder.* New York: Macmillan Publishing Co., 1988.

Games

Arnold, Arnold. *The World Book of Children's Games.* New York: World Book, 1972.

Blake, Quentin, Fulvio Testa, et al. *The Fantastic Book of Board Games.* New York: St. Martin's Press, 1988.

Brinckloe, Julie. *Playing Marbles.* New York: William Morrow & Co., 1978.

Ferretti, F. *The Great American Book of Sidewalk, Stoop, Dirt Curb and Alley Games.* New York: Workman Publishing Co., 1975.

Frankel, Lillian, and Godfrey Frankel. *101 Best Nature Games and Projects.* New York: Grammercy, 1969.

Gallagher, Rachel. *Games in the Street.* New York: Four Winds Press, 1975.

Gregson, Bob. *The Incredible Indoor Games Book.* Belmont, CA: David S. Lake Publishers, 1982.

————. *Outrageous Indoor Games.* Belmont, CA: David S. Lake Publishers, 1984.

Grunfeld, Frederic. *Games of the World.* New York: Holt, Rinehart & Winston, 1975.

Kamiya, Art. *Elementary Teacher's Handbook of Indoor and Outdoor Games.* West Nyack, NY: Parker Publishing Company, 1985.

Langstaff, John, and Carol Langstaff. *Shimmy Shimmy Coke-Ca-Pop.* New York: Doubleday, 1973.

McLenighan, Valjean. *International Games.* Milwaukee: Raintree Publishers, 1978.

Orlick, Terry. *The Cooperative Sports and Games Book.* New York: Pantheon Books, 1978.

Rockwell, Anne. *Games (and How To Play Them).* New York: Thomas Y. Crowell, 1973.

Vinton, Iris. *The Folkways Omnibus of Children's Games.* Harrisburg, PA: Stackpole Books, 1970.

Nature

Allison, Linda. *The Sierra Club Summer Book.* Updated Compendium. Boston: Sierra Club Books/ Little, Brown & Co., 1989.

————. *The Wild Inside.* Boston: Sierra Club Books/Little, Brown & Co., 1988.

Anderson, Madelyn. *New Zoos.* New York: Franklin Watts, 1987.

Arnold, Caroline. *Dinosaur Mountain: Graveyard of the Past.* New York: Clarion Books, 1989.

————. *Trapped in Tar: Fossils from the Ice Age.* New York: Clarion Books, 1987.

Arnosky, Jim. *Sketching Outdoors in Spring.* New York: Lothrop, Lee & Shepard Books, 1986.

Bellamy, David. *The Forest.* New York: Clarkson N. Potter, 1988.

Bernstein, Bonnie, and Leigh Blair. *Native American Crafts Workshop.* Belmont, CA: David S. Lake Publishers, 1982.

Bjork, Christina, and Lena Anderson. *Linea's Windowsill Garden.* New York: Farrar, Straus & Giroux, 1988.

Brandenberg, Franz. *Leo and Emily's Zoo.* New York: Greenwillow Books, 1988.

Cochrane, Jennifer. *Urban Ecology.* New York: Bookwright Press, 1988.

Cohen, Joy. *Going Green: A Kid's Handbook for Saving the Planet.* New York: Penguin, 1990.

Cowcher, Helen. *Rainforests.* New York: Farrar, Straus & Giroux, 1988.

Dennis, John. *Summer Bird Feeding.* Elgin, IL: Prism Creative Group, 1980.

Edlin, Herbert. *The Illustrated Encyclopedia of Trees.* New York: Crown Publishers, 1978.

Eriksson, Paul. *The Bird Finder's 3-Year Notebook.* Middlebury, VT: Paul S. Eriksson, 1980.

Feeney, Stephanie, and Ann Fielding. *Sand and Sea: Marine Life of Hawaii.* Honolulu: University of Hawaii Press, 1989.

George, Jean C. *One Day in the Tropical Rainforest.* New York: Thomas Y. Crowell, 1990.

————. *One Day in the Prairie.* New York: Thomas Y. Crowell, 1987.

Haas, Carolyn Buhai, Ann Cole, and Barbara Naftzger. *Backyard Vacation.* Boston: Little, Brown & Co., 1980.

Jaspersohn, William. *How the Forest Grew.* New York: Greenwillow Books, 1980.

Kohl, Herbert, and Judith Kohl. *The View from the Oak.* New York: Charles Scribner's Sons, 1977.

Lampton, Christopher. *Endangered Species.* New York: Franklin Watts, 1988.

Lavies, Bianca. *Lily Pad Pond and Tree Trunk Traffic.* New York: Dutton, 1989.

Lerner, Carol. *Flowers of a Woodland Spring.* New York: William Morrow & Co., 1989.

————. *On the Forest Edge.* New York: William Morrow & Co., 1978.

————. *Plant Families.* New York: William Morrow & Co., 1989.

————. *Seasons of the Tall Grass Prairie.* New York: William Morrow & Co., 1980.

Lyon, George Ella. *A B Cedar: An Alphabet of Trees.* Boston: Little, Brown & Co., 1989.

Marshall, Janet Perry. *My Camera: At the Aquarium.* Boston: Little, Brown & Co., 1989.

McVey, Vicki. *The Sierra Club Wayfinding Book.* Boston: Sierra Club Books/Little, Brown & Co., 1989.

Milford, Susan. *The Kids' Nature Book.* Charlotte, VT: Williamson Publishing Co., 1989.

Miller, Christina, and Louise Berry. *Coastal Rescue: Preserving Our Seashores.* New York: Atheneum Publishers, 1989.

Milton, Joyce. *Whales: The Gentle Giants.* New York: Random House, 1989.

Narahaski, Keiko. *I Have a Friend.* New York: Mc-Elderry Books, 1987.

Patent, Dorothy. *Looking at Dolphins and Porpoises.* New York: Holiday House, 1989.

————. *Where the Bald Eagles Gather.* New York: Clarion Books, 1984.

————. *The Whooping Crane, a Comeback Story.* New York: Clarion Books, 1988.

Petrides, George. *Peterson Field Guides: Trees and Shrubs.* Boston: Houghton Mifflin Co., 1986.

Pooley, Sarah. *A Day of Rhymes.* New York: Alfred A. Knopf, 1987.

Pope, Joyce. *Seashores.* New Jersey: Troll Associates, 1990.

Robbins, Ken. *Beach Days.* New York: Viking, 1987.

Rowland-Entwistle, Theodore. *Jungles and Rainforests.* New York: Silver, Burdett & Ginn, 1987.

Ryden, Hope. *America's Bald Eagle.* New York: The Putnam Berkley Group, 1985.

Rylant, Cynthia. *Henry and Midge and the Forever Sea.* New York: Bradbury Press, 1989.

Shedd Aquarium Staff. *Aquatic Life in the John G. Shedd Aquarium.* Chicago: Shedd Aquarium Society, 1983.

Simon, Seymour. *How To Be an Ocean Scientist in Your Own Home.* New York: J. B. Lippincott Co., 1988.

Udry, Janice May. *A Tree Is Nice.* New York: Harper & Row, 1987.

Venning, Frank. *Wildflowers of North America.* New York: Golden Press, 1984.

Waters, Maryjane. *The Victory Garden Kids' Book: A Beginner's Guide to Growing Fruits and Flowers.* New York: Houghton Mifflin Co., 1988.

White, Sandra Sterling, and Michael Filisky. *The Rescue of a Baby Harbor Seal.* New York: Crown Publishers, 1989.

Ziter, Cary. *When Turtles Come to Town.* New York: Franklin Watts, 1989.

Newsletters and Magazines

American Association for Gifted Children, 15 Grammercy Park, New York, NY 10003.

Chickadee, P.O. Box 11314, Des Moines, IA 50340.

Children's Magazine Guide, R. R. Bowker, 245 W. 17th Street, New York, NY 10011.

Cobblestone, 30 Grove Street, St. Peterborough, NH 03458.

Copycat Magazine, P.O. Box 081546, Racine, WI 53408-1546.

Cricket, P.O. Box 52961, Boulder, CO 80322-2961.

The Five Owls, 2004 Sheridan Avenue South, Minneapolis, MN 55405.

Gifted Children Monthly, 213 Hollydell Drive, Sewell, NJ 08080.

Growing Child, P.O. Box 620, Lafayette, IN 47902.

Kid City, 200 Watt Street, P.O. Box 53349, Boulder, CO 80322.

The Kobrin Letter, 732 Greer Road, Palo Alto, CA 94303.

Mother Earth News: Almanac of Family Play, P.O. Box 70, Hendersonville, NC 28791.

National Association for Gifted Children, 4175 Lovell Road, Suite 140, Circle Pines, MN 55014.

National Geographic World, 17th and M Streets NW, Washington, DC 20036.

Odyssey, 1027 N. 7th Street, Milwaukee, WI 53233.

Parent and Preschooler, Preschool Publications, P.O. Box 1851, Garden City, NY 11530.

Parents' Choice: A Review of Children's Media, Box 185, Waban, MA 02168.

Penny Power, P.O. Box 54861, Boulder, CO 80322-4861.

School-Age Notes, P.O. Box 120674, Nashville, TN 37212.

Sports Illustrated for Kids, P.O. Box 830609, Birmingham, AL 35283-0609.

3-2-1 Contact, P.O. Box 53051, Boulder, CO 80322-3051.

World Council for Gifted and Talented Children, Box 218, Teacher's College, Columbia University, 525 W. 120st Street, New York, NY 10027.

Yellow Brick Road, 3940 Natchez Avenue South, St. Louis Park, MN 55416.

For Parents and Teachers

Alvino, James. *Parents' Guide to Raising a Gifted Child.* Boston: Little, Brown & Co., 1985.

Asimov, Isaac. *Asimov's Biographical Encyclopedia of Science and Technology.* New York: Doubleday, 1982.

Binkley, Marilyn. *Becoming a Nation of Readers: What Parents Can Do.* Washington, DC: U.S. Department of Education, 1988.

Burns, Marilyn. *Everykid's Book of Things To Do.* New York: Bantam Books, 1979.

Cascare, Andrea. *Good Books To Grow On.* New York: Warner Books, 1985.

Children's Book Council, 67 Irving Place, New York, NY 10003.

Cole, Ann, Carolyn Haas, and Betty Weinberger. *Purple Cow to the Rescue.* Boston: Little, Brown & Co., 1982.

Cole, Ann, Carolyn Haas, Elizabeth Heller, and Betty Weinberger. *Children Are Children Are Children.* Boston: Little, Brown & Co., 1978.

Durkin, Lisa Lyons. *Special Times for Parents and Kids Together.* New York: Warner Books, 1987.

Elkind, David. *The Hurried Child Growing Up Too Fast Too Soon.* Reading, MA: Addison-Wesley Publishing Co., 1981.

Haas, Carolyn Buhai. *The Big Book of Fun.* Chicago: Chicago Review Press, 1988.

Haas-Foletta, Karen, and Michelle Cogley. *School-Age Activities for After School Children.* Nashville: School-Age Notes, 1990.

Haviland, Virginia. *Children's Literature: A Guide to Reference Sources.* Washington, DC: Library of Congress, 1982.

Jordan, Dorothy Ann, and Marjorie Adoff Cohen. *Great Vacations with Your Kids.* New York: Dutton, 1987.

Kinghorn, Harriet, and Fay Hill Smith. *At Day's End: Book-Related Activities for Small Groups.* Englewood, CO: Libraries Unlimited, 1989.

Kobrin, Beverly. *Eyeopeners: How To Use Children's Books About Real People.* New York: Penguin, 1989.

Landin, Les, and Frank Tribault. *Creative Chalkboard Activities.* Belmont, CA: David S. Lake Publishers, 1986.

Lansky, Vicky. *Birthday Parties.* Deephaven, MN: The Book Peddlers, 1989.

Larrick, Nancy. *A Parent's Guide to Children's Reading.* New York: The Westminster/John Knox Press, 1983.

LaShan, Eda. *The Conspiracy Against Childhood.* New York: Atheneum Publishers, 1980.

Marzollo, Jean. *The New Kindergarten.* New York: Harper & Row, 1987.

———. *Superkids: Creative Learning Activities for Children 5–15.* New York: Harper & Row, 1981.

McCoy, Elin. *Year-Round Playbook.* New York: Random House, 1979.

Michaelis, Bill, and Dolores Michaelis. *Learning Through Noncompetitive Activities and Play.* Belmont, CA: David S. Lake Publishers, 1979.

Oppenheim, Joanne. *Choosing Books.* New York: Ballantine Books, 1986.

Osband, Gillian. *What Can I Do Indoors?* London: Hodder and Stoughton, 1983.

Paul, Aileen. *Kids Camping.* New York: Doubleday, 1973.

Peet, Bill. *Bill Peet: An Autobiography.* Boston: Houghton Mifflin Co., 1987.

Portnoy, Sanford, and Joan Sanford. *How To Take Great Trips with Your Kids.* Boston: The Harvard Common Press, 1983.

Rich, Dorothy. *Success for Children.* Washington, DC: The Home and School Institute, 1972.

Rollack, Jane. *Public Library Services for Children.* Hamden, CT: The Shoe String Press, 1989.

Russell, William. *Classics To Read Aloud to Your Children.* New York: Crown Publishers, 1984.

Saunders, Jacqulyn, and Pamela Espeland. *Bringing Out the Best.* Minneapolis: Free Spirit Publishing, 1986.

Schon, Isabel. *Basic Collection of Books in Spanish.* New York: Scarecrow Press, 1986.

Staff of *Weekly Reader. 60 Years of News for Kids.* New York: World Almanac Books, 1988.

Stangl, Jean. *Magic Mixtures: Creative Fun for Little Ones.* Belmont, CA: David S. Lake Publishers, 1986.

Sutherland, Zena. *The Best in Children's Books, (1979–1984).* Chicago: University of Chicago Press, 1987.

———. *Children and Books.* 7th ed. Glenview, IL: Scott, Foresman & Co., 1986.

Thomas, Dian. *Roughing It Easy: A Unique Idea Book for Camping and Cooking.* Provo, UT: Brigham Young Press, 1974.

Trelease, Jim. *The Read-Aloud Handbook.* New York: Penguin, 1985.

Vance, Eleanor. *The Everything Book.* New York: Western Publishing Co., 1974.

Wilms, Denise. *Science Books for Children.* Chicago: American Library Association, 1985.

Poems

Jackson, David. *The Way to the Zoo: Poems About Animals.* London: Oxford University Press, 1989.

Janeczko, Paul. *This Delicious Day: 65 Poems.* New York: Orchard Books, 1987.

McCarthy, Patricia. *Animals Galore!* New York: Dial, 1989.

Merriam, Eve. *Fresh Paint.* New York: Macmillan Publishing Co., 1987.

Prelutsky, Jack, ed. *Poems by A. Nonny Mouse.* New York: Alfred A. Knopf, 1989.

Singer, Marilyn. *Turtle in July.* New York: Macmillan Publishing Co., 1989.

Whipple, Laura, ed. *Eric Carle's Animals.* New York: Philomel Books, 1989.

Williams, Helen. *In Abigail's Garden.* New York: Dutton, 1987.

———. *The Language of Flowers.* New York: Dutton, 1988.

Publishing

Aliki. *How a Book Is Made.* New York: Harper & Row, 1986.

Fleming, Thomas. *Behind the Headlines.* New York: Walker & Co., 1989.

Gibbons, Gail. *Deadline! From News to Newspaper.* New York: Thomas Y. Crowell, 1987.

Thomson, Ruth. *Making a Book.* New York: Franklin Watts, 1988.

Science

Alesse, Craig. *Don't Take My Picture! How To Take Fantastic Photos of Family and Friends (and Have Fun!).* Amherst, NY: Amherst Media, 1990.

Alexander, Alison, and Susie Bower. *Science Magic.* New York: Prentice Hall, 1986.

Aliki. *Digging Up Dinosaurs.* New York: Thomas Y. Crowell, 1981.

Baum, Arline, and Joseph Baum. *Opt: An Illusionary Tale.* New York: Viking, 1987.

Blackwelder, Sheila K. *Science for All Seasons.* New York: Prentice Hall, 1980.

Booth, Jerry. *The Big Beast Book: Dinosaurs and How They Got That Way.* Boston: Little, Brown & Co., 1989.

Boyne, Walter. *The Smithsonian Book of Flight for Young People.* New York: Aladdin Books, 1988.

Bramley, Franklyn. *What Happened to the Dinosaurs?* New York: Thomas Y. Crowell, 1989.

Center for Marine Conservation. *The Ocean Book: Aquarium and Seaside Activities for All Ages.* New York: John Wiley & Sons, 1990.

Cobb, Vicki. *Science Experiments You Can Eat.* New York: J. B. Lippincott Co., 1985.

Cole, Joanna. *The Magic School Bus at the Waterworks.* New York: Scholastic, 1987.

Czerkes, Stephen, and Sylvia Czerkes. *My Life with the Dinosaurs.* New York: Simon & Schuster, 1989.

50 Simple Things You Can Do To Save the Earth. Berkeley: Earthworks, 1989.

Fradin, Dennis. *Archaeology.* Chicago: Childrens Press, 1983.

Gibbons, Gail. *Catch the Wind! All About Kites.* Boston: Little, Brown & Co., 1989.

————. *Weather Forecasting.* New York: Four Winds Press, 1987.

Haas, Jessie. *The Sixth Sense and Other Stories.* New York: Greenwillow Books, 1988.

Hackwell, John W. *Digging to the Past: Excavations in Ancient Lands.* New York: Charles Scribner's Sons, 1987.

Hunt, Leslie. *Twenty-Five Kites That Fly.* New York: Dover Publications, 1971.

Jonas, Ann. *Reflections.* New York: Greenwillow Books, 1987.

Kohl, Herbert. *Mathematical Puzzlements.* New York: Schocken Books, 1987.

Koral, April. *Our Global Greenhouse.* New York: Franklin Watts, 1989.

Landt, Dennis. *Catch the Wind: A Book of Windmills and Windpower.* New York: Macmillan Publishing Co., 1984.

Lansky, Vicky. *The Taming of the Candy Monster.* Rev. ed. Wayzata, MN: Meadowbrook Press, 1978.

Macaulay, David. *The Way Things Work.* Boston: Houghton Mifflin Co., 1988.

Markle, Susan. *Exploring Summer: A Season of Science Activities, Puzzles, Games.* New York: Atheneum Publishers, 1987.

————. *Science Mini-Mysteries: Easy-To-Do Experiments Designed To Keep You Guessing.* New York: Atheneum Publishers, 1988.

Marlen, Paul D. *Messengers to the Brain: Our Fabulous Five Senses.* Washington, DC: National Geographic Society, 1984.

Newman, Lee, and Jay Newman. *Kitecraft.* New York: Crown Publishers, 1974.

Niles, Eldridge, Gregory Niles, and Douglas Niles. *The Fossil Factory.* Reading, MA: Addison-Wesley Publishing Co.,1989.

Oakley, Graham. *Graham Oakley's Magical Changes.* New York: Aladdin Books, 1987.

Ontario Science Center. *Scienceworks.* Reading, MA: Addison-Wesley Publishing Co., 1986.

Reed, Don. *The Dolphins and Me.* Boston: Sierra Club Books/Little, Brown & Co., 1989.

Ride, Sally, and Susie Okie. *To Space and Back.* New York: Lothrop, Lee & Shepard Books, 1986.

Sattler, Helen. *The Illustrated Dinosaur Dictionary.* New York: Lothrop, Lee & Shepard Books, 1983.

————. *Tyrannosaurus Rex and Its Kin: The Mesozoic Monsters.* New York: Lothrop, Lee & Shepard Books, 1989.

Schwartz, Henry. *How I Captured a Dinosaur.* New York: Orchard Books, 1989.

Simon, Seymour. *How To Be an Ocean Scientist in Your Own Home.* New York: J. B. Lippincott Co., 1988.

————. *The Optical Illusion Book.* New York: William Morrow & Co., 1984.

————. *Volcanoes and Storms.* New York: William Morrow & Co., 1989.

Smithsonian Family Learning Activities: Science Calendars. New York: GMG Publishing Corp., 1980.

Sullivan, George. *Treasure Hunt! The Sixteen-Year Search for the Lost Treasure Ship Atocha.* New York: Henry Holt & Co., 1987.

Tannenbaum, Beulah, and Harold Tannenbaum. *Making and Using Your Own Weather Station.* New York: Franklin Watts, 1989.

Testa, Fulvio. *If You Look Around You.* New York: Dutton, 1983.

Tyler, Jenny, and Graham Round. *Brain Puzzlers.* London: Usborne Publishing Ltd., 1980.

West, Dan. *The Day the TV Blew Up.* Racine, WI: Whitman, 1988.

Wilcox, Charlotte. *Trash!* Minneapolis: Carolrhoda Books, 1988.

Wyler, Rose. *Science Fun with a Homemade Chemistry Set.* New York: Julian Messner, 1987.

Zubrowski, Bernie. *Messing Around with Baking Chemistry.* Boston: Little, Brown & Co., 1981.